Complex Cooperation

Studies in Politics and Government

Books in the Studies in Politics and Government series are based on current research in political science. The series includes specialized research reports as well as monographs and edited volumes providing more comprehensive overwiews written for a larger audience of professionals, students and citizens sharing an interest in governmental and political affairs.

Previously published:

1. Raino Malnes and Arild Underdal (eds.):
   Rationality and Institutions
2. Peter M. Haas, Helge Hveem (ed.), Robert O. Keohane and Arild Underdal:
   Complex Cooperation
3. Bjørn Erik Rasch og Knut Midgaard (red.):
   Representativt demokrati. Spilleregler under debatt

Peter M. Haas, Helge Hveem (ed.),
Robert O. Keohane and Arild Underdal

Complex Cooperation

Institutions and Processes in
International Resource Management

Scandinavian University Press
Oslo

Scandinavian University Press (Universitetsforlaget AS),
P.O. Box 2959 Tøyen, N-0608 Oslo, Norway
Fax +47 22 57 53 53

Stockholm office
SCUP, Scandinavian University Press
P.O. Box 3255,
S-103 65 Stockholm, Sweden
Fax +46 8 20 99 82

Copenhagen Office
Scandinavian University Press AS
P.O. Box 54, DK-1002 København K, Denmark
Fax +45 33 32 05 70

© Scandinavian University Press (Universitetsforlaget AS) 1994

ISBN 82-00-03912-9

(Published with grants from the Department of Political science, University of
Oslo, and Centre for Development and the Environment, University of Oslo.)

Cover design: Harald Gulli
Printed in Norway by Edgar Høgfeldt AS, Kristiansand 1994

Contents

Interests, Property Rights, and Problems of Cooperation
Failing and facilitating international agreement in commodities   64
Helge Hveem

Measuring and Explaining Regime Effectiveness   92
Arild Underdal

Preface

The problem of cooperation in international relations never ceases to be important. Research on the integrative potential of different issueareas or segments and the history of cooperative attempts is therefore an attractive field. And the reality of both past and contemporary international politics and international political economy offers a true laboratory for interested researchers.

This book presents the views of four researchers who for some time, with partially overlapping perspectives and objects of study, have been preoccupied with such problems. It results directly from a symposium held in Tromsø, Norway, in June 1991. The brief exposés at the symposium and the exchange of views during discussions laid the foundation for the writing of the four reports. In the process, all authors were greatly helped by generous colleagues, some of whom participated in the symposium, and by their host institutions to complete their contributions amidst the normal rush of day-to-day business. They also exchanged comments and suggestions on their respective drafts. The four articles, although being individual reflections on a common theme, benefited from that exchange.

This modest editorial disclaimer does not, however, neglect the correspondence in theoretical perspective. All the contributions address the issue of what factors make cooperative efforts work, i.e. the issue of explaining cooperation or failure to cooperate. All are, although in varying degree, pursuing an eclectic road to theory-building. All see cooperative arrangements in a dynamic perspective, and several treat the issue of authority vs. market and the centralization – decentralization issue in considerable depth.

Keohane's article (Chapter 1) offers a broad approach in terms of issueareas covered. It follows mostly institutionalist perspectives and at the same time comes closest to advocating a parsimonious view of the cooperative optimum: a decentralized approach, favoring private property rights, that internalizes "the environmental costs of human action" may offer the most efficient strategy to environmental protection. Haas (Chapter 2) discusses structuralist, institutionalist, and cognitivist approaches to explaining cooperation on environment protection. His own study of the Mediterranean Action Plan shows that all three approaches are relevant in a dynamic analysis of the processes leading up to the plan, and he advocates an eclectic, non-parsimonious approach in attempting to construct a general theory. Hveem's article (Chapter 3), which differs from the other three in treating international commodity rather than environmental politics, follows a similar eclectic argument when explaining the failure of multilateral cooperative efforts in commodities, but ends by suggesting that institutionalist explanations, linked to property rights issues and the authority–market dimension, supplemented by cognitivist and structuralist perspectives account for most of the variance in the "success or failure" of commodity agreements. Underdal (Chapter 4) similarly addresses the causes of cooperative "success and failure", but in addition he devotes much of his contribution to conceptual groundwork for analyzing the effectiveness of cooperative efforts and, more than the other contributions, he addresses the issue of what makes cooperative arrangements actually work after having been agreed and formally set up. In doing so, he makes use of rational choice theories, although with some modifications. Finally, several of the articles address the question whether the explanation for cooperative "success" can be mostly or partly given in terms of an issue-area approach, asking whether certain problemareas represent more "benign" and others "malign" conditions for cooperation.

The book's ambition is to contribute to theorizing in an important field of both academic study and political action. The four contributions attempt to present a state-of-the-art and a synthesis of what the authors see as the more interesting and fruitful approaches in the literature. In doing this we have no ambition to cover the field exhaustively. It is our hope that the book will stimulate reflection and lead to more research – including further research by the authors themselves.

The editor wishes to express his gratitude and that of all the authors to the Norwegian Ministry of Foreign Affairs for financial support of the symposium, and to the Norwegian Council for Research and the Humanities (NAVF) for supporting the research project, of which this report is a part, as well as the publication of this report. Needless to say, neither of these institutions has any responsibility for the contents.

Helge Hveem

Against Hierarchy: An Institutional Approach to International Environmental Protection

Robert O. Keohane

Western political observers from the time of Thucydides have contrasted the hierarchy of authority characteristic of highly organized societies with the lack of hierarchical governance associated with interstate politics. Pericles, in his Funeral Oration as described by Thucydides, drew this contrast; so did Thomas Hobbes, the 17th-century philosopher and translator of Thucydides's great history of the Peloponnesian War. From the 17th century through the 20th, the institution of sovereignty both distinguished the internal from the external realm, and provided a justification for limiting intervention in the internal affairs of other states. As Martin Wight and the English School of international relations have shown, the function of the concept of sovereignty changed over time: "It began as a theory to justify the king being master in his new modern kingdom, absolute internally. Only subsequently was it turned outward to become the justification of equality of such sovereigns in the international community (Wight, 1992, pp. 2–3.)." By the 18th and 19th centuries, as Hedley Bull explains, the conception of sovereignty as reflecting equality and reciprocity had become the core principle of international society. The exchange of recognition of sovereignty had become "a basic rule of coexistence within the states system," from which could be derived corollaries such as the rule of non-intervention and the rights of states to domestic jurisdiction (Bull, 1977, pp. 34–37).[1]

While interdependence was low, sovereignty could provide the basis for a viable international system; as long as governments did not depend on others' decisions for their survival, they could afford to draw a strict distinction between internal and external politics, and refrain from extensive attempts to affect the internal policies of other states. Under these conditions, the institution of sovereignty served rulers' interests by restraining intervention, which could weaken the power of rulers over the ruled. Hence, agreement on principles of non-intervention represented a cartel-type solution to a problem of collective action; in specific situations, the dominant strategy was to intervene, but it made sense to refrain *conditional on others' restraint.*

High levels of interdependence call the sovereignty solution into question. Nuclear weapons pose one dimension of this problem: when decisions made elsewhere can destroy one's own country, or even the global environment, one can no longer be indifferent to the decision making processes in nuclear-armed states. Economic interdependence has also led governments to seek to affect the policies of others that were formerly regarded as domestic prerogatives, such as tariffs and monetary policy. Under conditions of high interdependence, the meaning of sovereignty changes. States no longer exert effective supremacy over what occurs within their territories; decisions are made by firms on a global basis, and other states' policies have major impacts within one's own boundaries. Instead, sovereignty confers legal authority that can either be exercised to the detriment of other states' interests, or be exchanged for influence over others' policies.[2]

When property resources are necessarily held in common, interdependence is high by definition: decisions by one state to appropriate, or degrade, common property resources affect everyone who might otherwise benefit by use of the resources in question. In his paper for this volume, Peter M. Haas points out that two-thirds of all international environmental regimes established since 1972 have involved common property resources. Hence, the traditional sovereignty-based solution, which assigns property rights to territorially based units, is inapplicable to these issues. Cooperative international action is necessary. That is, governments must adjust their policies to those of their partners; they must seek collective regulation.

This essay explores some features of such collective regulation. I argue first for decentralized, non-hierarchic modes of regulation, and explore some of the conditions that may facilitate the emergence of such organizational patterns. Then I consider the kinds of rules and property rights that are likely to be appropriate for international environmental protection, the role of consensual knowledge produced by "epistemic communities" (in Peter Haas's phrase), and the relationship between markets and environmental protection. I conclude by moving the analysis to the domestic level, inquiring about the relationship between international institutions and domestic politics in protection of the natural environment.

Non-hierarchic regulation: a real possibility

Regulation does not necessarily imply hierarchical rule on the analogy of domestic politics; we need to abandon this traditional domestic analogy if we are to devise institutions that facilitate international environmental cooperation. For the last decade, work on international cooperation and international regimes has sought to break down the dichotomy between domestic hierarchy and international anarchy by identifying the conditions under which international cooperation can occur and the roles that international institutions can play in facilitating such cooperation (Krasner, 1983; Keohane, 1984, 1989; Oye, 1986; Young, 1989). According to this institutionalist line of argument, cooperation requires common or complementary interests, and is facilitated by the existence of a relatively small number of key actors and by expectations that one's ability to gain others' cooperation in the future may be contingent on the degree of one's own accommodation in the present. Furthermore, cooperation typically requires alignment of mutual expectations and assurance of other states' commitment to particular courses of action. Policymakers always lack adequate information, and very high levels of uncertainty discourage the commitments upon which cooperation depends. Indeed, one of the major functions of international institutions in contemporary world politics is to provide information that reduces uncertainty and therefore helps to construct the basis for cooperation.

The international institutionalist approach to non-hierarchical cooperation has recently been powerfully reinforced by an independently produced line of argument about governing arrangements for common property resources. Common-pool resources (CPRs) are "sufficiently large natural or manmade resources that it is costly (but not impossible) to exclude potential beneficiaries from obtaining benefits from their use" (Gardner, Ostrom and Walker, 1990, p. 335). In her work on *Governing the Commons*, Elinor Ostrom begins by pointing out that, for many CPR problems, neither centralization of authority nor privatization is an effective response. Even if centralization is feasible within a society, unlike the situation in world politics, it may as often disrupt as reinforce effective social networks for resource management. Privatization is not a panacea because "in regard to nonstationary resources, such as water and fisheries, it is unclear what the establishment of private rights means ... even when particular rights are unitized, quantified, and salable, the resource *system* is still likely to be owned in common rather than individually" (Ostrom, 1990, p. 13).

Ostrom contends that commons problems can be dealt with more effectively by institutions involving relatively small numbers of actors and incorporating principles of reciprocity, than by either hierarchical external rule (as in Hobbes's *Leviathan*) or privatization. The key to such arrangements, both at the individual level, in irrigation or fisheries arrangements, and at the level of international environmental regimes, is providing incentives to participants to monitor each other's behavior and to respond to infractions. The principle of reciprocity in an organization such as the General Agreement on Tariffs and Trade (GATT) provides such incentives: countries whose products are discriminated against in trade have an incentive to use the GATT dispute-settlement procedures, both to achieve redress and to accumulate "bargaining chips" against attacks by others on their own protectionist policies. Indeed, reciprocity is a widespread practice both in small-scale common property regimes and in international relations, although hardly foolproof (Keohane, 1989, ch. 6, pp. 132–57; Ostrom, 1990).

For such procedures to work effectively, legal frameworks may be helpful (Tolba, 1990). It is important to recognize, however, that these legal frameworks will operate not as binding laws, but rather as sets of standards that facilitate the operation of reciprocity. Behavior will be ordered not through vertical hierarchy, but horizontally, through reciprocal mutual control. The international legal frameworks that emerge will have many loopholes, as the GATT dispute-settlement procedure does; but even legal frameworks with many loopholes, as in GATT, can create relations of reciprocity that promote compliance.[3] Such reciprocity facilitated the operation of the Mediterranean Action Plan, although it did not necessarily play a decisive role (P. Haas, 1990, p. 183).

Hence, the "tragedy of the commons" (Hardin, 1968) does not follow deterministically from the coexistence of common property resources and the absence of centralized rule (Ostrom, 1992). Indeed, it would be a tragedy if people believed the "tragedy of the commons" argument that horizonal ordering – cooperation through reciprocity – is impossible. On the contrary, Ostrom has shown that it is possible. Decentralized structures of enforceable authority do not deterministically or fatalistically doom attempts at cooperation. Behavior depends also on the nature of the institutions that human beings devise; in particular, whether these institutions provide incentives for rational but largely self-interested individuals to behave in ways consistent with the welfare of others. The institutional feature may be an "invisible hand," as in the thought of Adam Smith (1776); a "visible hand," as in Alfred Chandler's discussion of the managerial corporation (Chandler, 1977); or a shadowy presence, as in Robert Axelrod's "shadow of the future," which may be darkened or lengthened by institutions (Axelrod, 1984). Whatever its form, successful institutionalization will affect incentives in a way that leads people to behave consistently with the goals of the institution-builders.

Conditions for non-hierarchic regulation

We know less than we would like to about the conditions under which non-hierarchic regulation can thrive. Common interests are crucial; without these, there is little reason to believe that cooperation will occur. Actors must believe that they can make future gains through cooperation. The capacity to monitor the behavior of others is also essential; without such capacity, actors cannot respond conditionally to others' behavior, and reciprocity cannot work. For almost half a century, international regimes designed to limit discharges from oil tankers at sea were ineffective because compliance with their rules could not be monitored effectively – the sea was vast and surveillance technology primitive. Only when pollution-controlling equipment technologies were invented, and mandated for new shipbuilding, were these monitoring problems overcome. Monitoring whether new vessels had the requisite technology was easy; and, once the technology was in place, tanker captains had no incentive not to use it (Mitchell, 1993).

Although a single dominant power may be helpful in building institutions, it is not essential. However, the number of actors that can achieve gains through collaboration among themselves must be small enough, given monitoring and interacting capabilities, to be able to observe each other's behavior and target their reactions on particular states (Snidal, 1985). Otherwise, familiar problems of collective action will bedevil attempts at cooperation.

It is a platitude that whether institutions can develop may

depend on "structural" conditions, such as the distribution of power among actors. But we should also notice that these structural conditions of cooperation themselves depend in part on institutions. How large the key group (or "k-group") of cooperating actors can be depends, as noted in the previous paragraph, on their ability to monitor and target each other's behavior; but this ability itself depends in part on whether institutions exist that set standards, provide for transparency of policy through the exchange of information, or designate organizations (such as the International Atomic Energy Agency) as having the function of inspecting facilities run by states.

Another important factor affecting the likelihood and extent of international cooperation on environmental issues concerns the complex of interests involved in the situation. In "coordination games" there are multiple equilibria (Martin, 1992). Actors may have different preferences among these points; but some of them are superior to others for all actors. Once an equilibrium is reached, no actor has an incentive to defect unilaterally (the definition of an equilibrium); hence such agreements are self-enforcing. The problem is to share information and to coordinate action in such a way as to reach new equilibria that are better for all actors than the status quo. Coordinated standards of radio communication and international air transport lanes illustrate this type of situation.

Sustained cooperation is more difficult in "collaboration games," which have suboptimal equilibria. That is, all parties would be better off pursuing a different combination of policies, but agreements to pursue such policies are not self-executing. They are not equilibria; actors have incentives to defect from these agreements. The famous game of "Prisoners' Dilemma" when infinitely or indefinitely repeated is a collaboration game. Each prisoner has an incentive in each move to defect, since defecting against a cooperating player yields the highest payoff, and defecting against a defecting player limits one's losses. However, the equilibrium of mutual defection is worse for both players than mutual cooperation.

Collaboration games are common on international environmental issues involving common property resources. Politicians would prefer that their individual constituents breathe clean air, but that industries in their countries not become less competitive because of costly pollution control regulations. Everyone in the world will benefit from a more intact ozone layer but, insofar as substitutes for chlorofluorocarbons (CFCs) are costly, everyone would also prefer that others bear the burdens of substitution. In general, collective action problems are similar in structure to n-person prisoners' dilemmas (Hardin, 1982): they do not have self-enforcing Pareto-optimal equilibria.

International institutions perform different functions in coordination and collaboration games. In coordination games, it is sufficient to locate and publicize a salient point for mutual action: learning that other states will coordinate around that point, each government has an incentive to do the same. Collaboration games, by contrast, require more extensive arrangements for monitoring others' behavior and for excluding from the benefits of cooperation actors that fail to obey the rules, as the Montreal Protocol provides for trade discrimination against states that seek to "free-ride" on others' efforts to reduce CFC production. Reciprocity is crucial in collaboration games; institutions are needed that facilitate its operation.

International cooperation on common property resources is likely to be affected by the *sequence* of action. Research on both international relations and CPRs has shown that it is easier to gain agreement within small groups than among many actors. This is especially true if members of the smaller groups have more similar interests and perceptions than the wider set of actors. However, solving a problem may require wide agreement. The strategic difficulty posed by this conundrum is that securing agreement within a small group (among one's "allies") can under some conditions make getting wider consensus more difficult, as issues as diverse as Germany's "blank check" to Austria in 1914, or the difficulties with EC agricultural policies in the Uruguay Round trade talks, illustrate. On the other hand, the bargaining incentives to reach agreement within one's coalition are substantial. *Sequence* therefore becomes important, as any negotiator knows. It would be useful to have more systematic theoretical and empirical knowledge about the impact of sequencing on ultimate outcomes, especially under conditions of bounded rationality and uncertainty (Sebenius, 1984, 1991).

International cooperation on common property resources may or may not be promoted by linkages of these issues to other questions. During the last decade, the United States has sought unilaterally to achieve certain conservation goals – relating to fisheries, protection of marine mammals such as dolphins, and avoidance of "environmental flight" of polluting industries to Mexico – by linking these issues to commercial trade or, in the case of Mexico, to the North American Free Trade Area (NAFTA). If there is "slack" in the system, because a state is not taking full advantage of its bargaining power, such linkages may promote environmental goals. But they can backfire, either on the issue to which they are linked, or on relations more generally. Governments that are vulnerable to linkages may react by investing in greater independence, making the exercise of influence more difficult the next time around.

Another sort of linkage takes place not across issue areas but over time: accommodation by one state now becomes connected to accommodation by another state in the future. In Prisoners' Dilemma, this "shadow of the future" works in favor of cooperation. But in other games, such as Chicken, concern about one's future reputation can lead to tougher strategies. Furthermore, in real world politics, the games do not necessarily remain the same; a state may resist cooperation in the present if it will provide greater gains to its partners than to itself, *and* if those gains can potentially be transformed into the ability to change the nature of the relationship (the "game") to the disadvantage of the first state (Grieco, 1988; Powell, 1991; Keohane, 1992). We cannot automatically assume that long time horizons and long memories promote cooperation; we need to study more carefully the conditions under which this, or the opposite, is so.

Existing cooperative relationships can also be disrupted from outside. Ostrom shows how the failure of central governments to understand and enforce locally constructed arrangements of reciprocity made rational exploitation of fisheries and water resources in Sri Lanka more difficult (Ostrom, 1990, pp. 149–73). The analogy in international relations would be inappropriately ambitious global attempts at uniform regulation, which could make it more rather than less difficult for regional environmental protection arrangements to be developed or maintained.

Rules and property rights

To achieve effective international environmental cooperation, it is particularly important to focus on the question of the substantive property rights and rules that international regimes establish. Problems are solved by international regimes largely by creating rights and rules; as Oran Young has argued, "the core of every international regime is a cluster of rights and rules, [whose] exact content is a matter of intense interest to these actors" (Young, 1989, p. 15). People who construct regimes have purposes in doing so, and the rights and rules of regimes reflect visions of what sorts of behavior should be encouraged or proscribed. International regimes vary in their purposes even within issue areas, as the contrast between GATT's espousal of non-discriminatory trade and UNCTAD's emphasis on special privileges for developing countries (which prevailed up to a point in the 1970s) illustrates. It would be quite possible for international regimes to develop that were ostensibly designed to provide environmental protection but that actually protected polluting industries against prosecution, or that, like specialized agencies of the United Nations system such as FAO, acted largely as organizational sinecures for highly paid officials.

For decades, rules for oil tankers were in effect written by the oil transportation industry; the agricultural chemical industry is now seeking to write rules controlling exports of its products, and the US electric power industry is a principal opponent of binding rules to reduce emissions of greenhouse gases. "Capture" of international environmental institutions by laggard governments, the regulated industries themselves, or self-serving bureaucrats is a continual danger, especially in view of the weak systems of accountability characteristic of the United Nations system.

On economic, political, and ecological grounds, advocates of international environmental protection would be well advised, in my view, to try to establish a small set of principles and rules to which governments and international organizations could be held accountable, rather than to promulgate detailed rules prescribing specific actions for a wide variety of commons problems. In the first place, our knowledge changes so fast that it makes more sense to specify rather general goals (e.g. reduce anthropocentric sources of climate change) rather than specific (reduce CO_2 emissions by 30 percent in 10 years). We now know that many substances other than CO_2 affect global climate change; hence, had CO_2 rules been locked into place five years ago, the result might be either inefficient policy or widespread non-compliance.

Secondly, from a political standpoint, two major roles of international institutions are to increase concern about international environmental issues, through making them salient to public opinion, and to facilitate contracting through reducing transactions costs – the costs of making, monitoring, and enforcing contracts (Haas, Keohane, and Levy, 1993). It is much easier to focus public attention on a small number of goals than on detailed technical means; and it is easier to hold governments politically accountable for meeting a small number of general standards than many detailed regulations. The GATT system of general rules, with panels for dispute settlement to decide on the applicability of those rules to particular cases, makes much more sense than trying to write rules for a large number of eventualities.

The rules devised in international conferences, and embodied in international institutions, cannot be enforced hierarchically. Government enforcement is often a flawed strategy even within domestic society; without a world government, such a strategy is vacuous at the international level. The *Leviathan* approach will not work. Under some conditions, privatization may work; for instance, tax policies that eliminate incentives to pollute at the expense of society (the "polluter pays principle") are helpful where property rights can be assigned, as in the case of fixed-site sources of pollution. Nevertheless, as Ostrom emphasizes, privatization will not solve problems of common property resources.

Nor should we expect a single global architecture for institutions. An institutional approach to problems of international cooperation emphasizes both that the proximate interests (the incentives) of actors are affected by institutional conditions, and that institutions, if they are to work, must be consistent with the prior, more fundamental, interests of participants, as well as with their understandings of social reality. It is therefore important to encourage participants in a resource system involving goods that are not "site-bound" in Helge Hveem's terminology in this volume – such as appropriators of a commons resource such as fisheries, or sources of pollution and victims of it in a river basin system – to work out standards and monitoring and enforcement regulations that are suitable to their political and cultural as well as natural environmental conditions. It is much easier to do this where there are a few key actors who know each other than when many participants interact in an impersonal system. But, in the latter case, organizing participants into subgroups may permit cooperation among these subgroups. Likewise, on an international level it may be feasible to use what Herbert Simon (1969) has called "decomposable hierarchies" to facilitate a combination of decentralization and overall coordination.

Social learning and epistemic communities

Ernst Haas (1990) has emphasized, in his important and creative work, the importance of consensual knowledge for international organizations; Peter Haas has developed this theme in particularly interesting ways. As in his paper for this volume, Peter Haas stresses the role of epistemic communities: the communities of politically involved scientists that discover and promote consensual knowledge. These students of collective cognitive processes have much to teach us about sources of change in international politics. Indeed, realism, institutionalism, and the cognitive school are not so much competing paradigms as potentially complementary lines of argument, each emphasizing a different set of independent variables: interests and power for realism, information and institutional attributes for institutionalism, cognition and social learning for the cognitivists. As Peter Haas argues in his chapter for this volume, all have value. Since any theory has to choose which factors it will regard as variables, and which to select merely as constant background factors, it is perfectly reasonable for realists to select interests and power as their variables, taking institutional arrangements or international society as given. It is something else, however, to deny the impact of institutional factors altogether. Institutions are fundamental to human behavior because people orient their actions according to expectations and norms provided by conventions, informal and formal rules, and organizations; that is, in the context of institutions. Without institutions, there would be no society and no effective communication; force might be used, but political influence could not be exercised. The basic activities of international relations studied by realists would not exist.

Institutionalists seek to show realists both that institutions matter and that they vary sufficiently, over space and time, to become significant variables by which to understand international relations. Thus the critical question that institutionalists direct toward realists is one of sufficiency: granted that interests and power are important, what reason do we have to believe that they are the whole story – or close enough to the whole story for us to be able to omit other factors from our account?

Toward the cognitivists, institutionalists make a different inquiry. In the first place, empirical research indicates that epistemic communities have been more important on some issues than on others (Haas, 1992). It would be valuable to know to what extent these variations have their sources in institutional factors, in interests, and in power. Furthermore, when the activities of epistemic communities are politically significant, we still have to ask whether they are *endogenous* to patterns of interests, power, and institutions. After all, politicians and organizations approve research budgets and research programs, and they tend to structure the channels by which demands are heard by policymakers. Granting that the scientists make discoveries that are relevant to politics, and that they hold normative beliefs about how their scientific knowledge can be used, political leaders can still affect the direction of knowledge-creation through anticipating what kinds of research are likely to have favorable or unfavorable political implications, from their standpoints; and they can usually affect the composition of scientific committees that advise on policy issues. Insofar as political leaders are able to anticipate the political implications of scientific discoveries, they may be able to encourage or discourage the formation of epistemic communities; and those communities that do exist may act to some extent as their agents. Under such conditions, what appears to be a process of science-driven increases in consensual knowledge may have deeper sources in the classical political variables of interests, power, and institutional organization.

Environmental protection and markets

The content of the rights and rules of international regimes changes over time. Even if we understood why certain areas of activity are regulated while others are not, and the strength and scope of international regimes, we would not fully comprehend international regimes unless we had some insights into the purposes that they are meant to serve.

During the 1980s, international environmental protection was inscribed on the agenda of world political leaders, owing to a combination of public awareness and disturbing scientific discoveries. Yet, at the same time, market-oriented policies were reinforced and re-legitimated worldwide. A major question for the 1990s and the next century is whether a social consensus can be achieved that reconciles environmental protection with market-oriented economic practices; and whether such a consensus can be institutionalized internationally. Perhaps the most relevant analogy is with the period immediately after World War II, when a compromise was made between the social welfare state and liberal markets, a compromise that John Ruggie has called "embedded liberalism." In Ruggie's words, "movement toward greater openness in the international economy would be coupled with safeguards that acknowledged and even facilitated the interventionist character of the modern capitalist state" (Ruggie, 1991, p. 4).[4] This consensus, facilitated by the spread of Keynesian ideas, was institutionalized between 1944 and the end of the 1950s in a variety of international regimes – internationally agreed rules and practices governing economic transactions among market economy countries. These regimes included some elaborate organizations such as the International Monetary Fund and the World Bank, and ongoing rule-oriented negotiations, such as those sponsored by GATT. For more than 30 years, these institutions have helped to prevent the often-predicted reversion to trade blocs or trade wars.

These successful economic institutions were not hierarchical, but facilitated cooperation among states. They rested on norms and rules that accommodated both the institutions of the welfare state and the practices of liberal economic exchange. International arrangements to maintain currency convertibility, the GATT regime limiting the rights of states to impose restrictions on trade, and international legal regimes providing for enforcement of contracts were in general consistent with market principles, albeit with some modifications and exceptions. Lending by the World Bank or the IMF to developing countries, or arrangements such as the Multifiber Arrangement in textile trade, alter market patterns of economic activity with the objective of fostering other values or promoting interests that might lose out in a free market. However, proposals for a New International Economic Order or for an authoritative regime to control extraction of seabed minerals, which would have supplanted market mechanisms with authoritative allocation, have not been successful, since they contradict hegemonic market principles supported by dominant powers.

Perhaps the most important question for the future of international environmental protection is whether a comparable compromise – normatively widely shared and organizationally decentralized – can be made between economic efficiency and competitiveness, and market principles, on the one hand; and environmental protection, on the other.

International institutions and domestic politics

Few people devote much effort to promoting the "global welfare," but many people care about environmental conditions in their own localities, and global environmental quality as it affects them. Thus to mobilize pressure for international regulation that enhances environmental protection, international institutions need to promote concern within societies about international rule-making. Effective international environmental institutions promote domestic political concern by scheduling agenda-setting public meetings, such as the UN Conference on Environment and Development in Rio de Janiero during June 1992, which provide opportunities for both criticism by nongovernmental organizations and attempts by governments to prove their environmental bona fides through making commitments. Conversely, the adverse publicity received by leaders who refrain from making such commitments, such as President George Bush at Rio, may help their "greener" adversaries at home.

A combination of international pressure and domestic environmentalism is crucial in putting pressure on laggards, such as the United States with respect to biodiversity and climate change at Rio. External pressure works best when there is a faction within the target government, or within a democratic society, favoring policy change.

While international institutions promote greater concern for the environment in both advanced industrial countries and developing countries, they also have to improve the capacity of governments in Asia, Africa, and Latin America to monitor and enforce environmental laws (Haas, Keohane, and Levy, 1993). Administrative structures in many of these countries are weak, and the economic incentives to seek competitiveness at the expense of the natural and human environments may seem compelling.

Within the context of special arrangements such as the proposed North American Free Trade Area (NAFTA), it may be feasible for countries with higher environmental standards such as the United States to put pressure on their partners with lower standards, such as Mexico. But, on most issues, what is needed instead is technical and financial support for capacity-building in the developing countries. Environmentalists in these countries need material resources, political support, and technical help in order both to increase the salience of environmental issues to their governments, and to ensure effective action on them. Yet, since money is fungible, there is a danger that funds provided from abroad for environmental protection will merely release resources within a developing country for other purposes; hence questions of what is known as "conditionality" in the IMF lexicon become important for the environment as well. A significant question that deserves research is how to design financial transfers to maximize the incentives for governments in the developing countries to act effectively on environmental problems.

Conclusion

The domestic analogy and discussions of the "tragedy of the commons" may have led some people to believe that international environmental protection should be fostered through the re-invention of Hobbes's *Leviathan*. In this model, international environmental law would be legislated, then enforced. But reflection on the nature of international relations suggests that such an organizational design would fail. World politics is inherently decentralized; any enforcement of rules that takes place is not managed from above but occurs through the operation of reciprocity among states, often with the active involvement of intergovernmental and nongovernmental organizations. If the international environment is to be protected through international action, the organizations that accomplish this task will not be patterned on modern states. Nor will the broader institutions, incorporating informal and formal rules, be enforced in a hierarchical manner.

Where property rights can be privatized in a way that provides incentives to internalize the environmental costs of human action, this strategy may provide the most efficient path to environmental protection. Markets should be modified to promote environmental quality whenever possible. Yet in many cases involving common property resources, full privatization will be impossible; collective management of resources will have to be carried out by institutions that foster both coordination and collaboration through reciprocity, monitoring, and persuasion. These institutions, to be legitimate, will have to be multilateral in form – to involve many states, and to operate according to non-discriminatory rules based on general principles (Ruggie, 1992). They will also have to "get the incentives right."

Finally, political pressure for environmental protection must continue to be mobilized at the domestic level, and both nongovernmental and governmental institutions need the capacity to analyze and implement protective policies. Without robust institutions at both domestic and international levels, linked closely to one another, diffuse public pressure for "green" policies could lead to merely symbolic efforts rather than to effective measures to assure continuing improvement of the quality of the natural and human environment.

Notes

1 Wight (1977, p. 135) makes this connection between sovereignty and reciprocity explicit by saying that "reciprocity was inherent in the Western conception of sovereignty."

2 This process of political exchange is illustrated by GATT dispute settlement on anti-dumping (AD) and countervailing duty (CVD) issues: "While de novo review of pure questions of law and of law-intensive mixed questions impinges upon U.S. sovereignty to some extent, that may be a price worth paying for reciprocal control over the AD/CVD determinations of nearly one hundred other countries" (Stuart, 1992, p. 751).

3 GATT dispute settlement operates on only a limited set of trade issues; much unilateral and bilateral activity is not regulated in formal institutional ways. However, within its limited sphere, GATT dispute settlement has a fairly impressive record of fostering compliance. See Hudec, Kennedy, and Sgarbossa (1993). During the 1980s, the United States was found in violation of GATT rules on 10 occasions; in 6 of those episodes it altered is administrative regulations or legislation in order to make its practices GATT-consistent (Keohane, in process, ch. 8).

4 See also Ruggie (1983). In this article, Ruggie acknowledges his debt to Fred Hirsch's "brilliant dissection of the social functions of inflation" (Hirsch, 1978, esp. p. 278).

References

Axelrod, Robert (1984) *The Evolution of Cooperation* (New York: Basic Books).

Bull, Hedley (1977) *The Anarchical Society* (New York: Columbia University Press).

Chandler, Alfred (1977) *The Visible Hand: The Managerial Revolution in American Business* (Cambridge, Mass.: Harvard University Press).

Gardner, Roy, Elinor Ostrom, and James Walker (1990) "The Nature of Common-Pool Resource Problems," *Rationality and Society*, vol. 2, pp. 335–58.

Grieco, Joseph (1988) "Anarchy and the Limits of Cooperation: A Realist Critique of the Newest Liberal Institutionalism," *International Organization*, vol. 42, no. 3 (Summer), pp. 485–508.

Haas, Ernst B. (1990) *When Knowledge is Power* (Berkeley: University of California Press).

Haas, Peter M. (1990) *Saving the Mediterranean* (New York: Columbia University Press).

Haas, Peter M., ed. (1992) *Knowledge, Power and International Policy Coordination*. *International Organization*, special issue, vol. 46, no. 1 (Winter).

Haas, Peter M., Robert O. Keohane, and Marc A. Levy, eds (1993) *Institutions for the Earth: Sources of Effective International Environmental Protection* (Cambridge, Mass.: MIT Press).

Hardin, Garrett (1968) "The Tragedy of the Commons." *Science*, vol. 162, pp. 1243–8.

Hardin, Russell (1982) *Collective Action* (Baltimore, Md: Johns Hopkins University Press for Resources for the Future).

Hirsch, Fred (1978) "The Ideological Underlay of Inflation," in P. Hirsch and John H. Goldthorpe, eds, *The Political Economy of Inflation* (Cambridge, Mass.: Harvard University Press).

Hobbes, Thomas (1651) *Leviathan* (Oxford: Blackwell, 1960).

Hudec, Robert E., Daniel L. M. Kennedy, and Mark Sgarbossa (1993) "A Statistical Profile of GATT Dispute Settlement Cases: 1948–1989," *Minnesota Journal of Global Trade*, vol. 2, no. 1 (Winter), pp. 1–113.

Keohane, Robert O. (1984) *After Hegemony: Cooperation and Discord in the World Political Economy* (Princeton, NJ: Princeton University Press).

Keohane, Robert O. (1989) *International Institutions and State Power* (Boulder, Colo.: Westview).

Keohane, Robert O. (1993) "Institutionalist Theory and the Realist Challenge after the Cold War," in David Baldwin, ed., *Neorealism and Neoliberalism: The Contemporary Debate* (New York: Columbia University Press).

Keohane, Robert O. (in process) *Contested Commitments in United States Foreign Policy, 1783–1989*.

Krasner, Stephen, ed. (1983) *International Regimes* (Ithaca, NY: Cornell University Press).

Martin, Lisa (1992) "Interests, Power and Multilateralism," *International Organization*, vol. 46, no. 4 (Autumn), pp. 765–92.

Mitchell, Ronald (1993) "International Oil Pollution of the Oceans," in P.M. Haas, R.O. Keohane and M.A. Levy, eds, *Institutions for the Earth*, (Cambridge, Mass.; MIT Press), ch. 5, pp. 183–248.

Ostrom, Elinor (1990) *Governing the Commons: The Evolution of Institutions for Collective Action* (Cambridge: Cambridge University Press).

Ostrom, Elinor (1992) "The Rudiments of a Theory of the Origins, Survival and Performance of Common-Property Institutions," in Daniel W. Bromley, ed., *Making the Commons Work: Theory, Practice and Policy* (San Francisco: Institute for Contemporary Studies).

Oye, Kenneth A., ed. (1986) *Cooperation Under Anarchy* (Princeton, NJ: Princeton University Press).

Powell, Robert (1991) "Absolute and Relative Gains in International Relations Theory," *American Political Science Review*, vol. 85, no. 4 (December), pp. 1303–20.

Ruggie, John Gerard (1983) "International Regimes, Transactions and Change: Embedded Liberalism in the Postwar Economic Order," in S. Krasner, ed, *International Regimes* (Ithaca, NY: Cornell University Press), pp. 195–231.

Ruggie, John Gerard (1991) "Embedded Liberalism Revisited: Progress in International Economic Relations," in Beverly Crawford and Emmanuel Adler, ed., *Progress in International Relations* (New York: Columbia University Press)

Ruggie, John Gerard (1992) "Multilateralism: The Anatomy of an Institution," *International Organization*, vol. 46, no. 3 (Summer), pp. 561–98.

Sebenius, James K. (1984) *Negotiating the Law of the Sea* (Cambridge, Mass.: Harvard University Press).

Sebenius, James K. (1991) "Designing Negotiations Toward a New Regime: The Case of Global Warming," *International Security*, vol. 15, no. 4 (Spring), pp. 110–48.

Simon, Herbert A. (1969) *The Sciences of the Artificial* (Cambridge, Mass.: MIT Press).

Smith, Adam (1776) *The Wealth of Nations* (Chicago: University of Chicago Press, bicentennial edition, 1976).

Snidal, Duncan (1985). "The Limits of Hegemonic Stability Theory," *International Organization*, vol. 39, no. 4 (Fall), pp. 579–614.

Stuart, Andrew W. (1992). "'I Tell Ya I don't get no Respect!': The Policies Underlying Standards for Review in U.S. Courts as a Basis for Deference to Municipal Determinations in GATT Panel Appeals,"

Law and Policy in International Business, vol. 23, no. 3 (Spring), pp. 749–790.

Tolba, Mustfa K. (1990) "Building an Environmental Institutional Framework for the Future," *Environmental Conservation*, vol. 17, no. 2 (Summer).

Wight, Martin (1977) *Systems of States* (Leicester: Leicester University Press).

Wight, Martin (1992) *International Theory: The Three Traditions* (New York: Holmes & Meier).

Young, Oran (1989) *International Cooperation: Building Regimes for Natural Resources and the Environment* (Ithaca, NY: Cornell University Press).

Regime Patterns for Environmental Management

Peter M. Haas

Transboundary pollution is now widely recognized as a threat to sustainable development. Yet, under what conditions do countries recognize new problems, and under what conditions are they capable of collectively responding in an effective way to these challenges? Without transcending the existing conditions of the international political system, what processes are available for the effective management of transboundary environmental problems? My intention in this essay is to explicate the patterns that theorists from different approaches predict in the sphere of international environmental regimes. By regime patterns I mean styles of collective management and lesson drawing associated with regime creation, persistence, and change.

Each of the three major schools of thought in current international relations literature predicts distinct patterns by which such cooperation may occur. Each school has partial empirical support for explanations falling within its domain, but none is sufficient to explain the full range of variation an analyst would desire. Shifts between the patterns are particularly intriguing to understand theoretically. Explanations based solely on power and circumstance (or issue structure) generally fail adequately to explain such change. This failing is a consequence of the limited assumptions about international behavior underlying each school's analysis of elements of a complex international system. The failure of each school is due not to the indeterminacy of the international system, although that is possible, but rather to the limited temporal and geographic scope of each theory.

Good theory requires theorists to make simplifying assumptions about the world. Yet, as John Ruggie and others have argued, most neorealist and institutionalist accounts of international cooperation are hindered by their focus on problems associated with the post-Westphalian international order. By not heeding the underlying dynamics that gave rise to such an order, Ruggie contends that these theorists neglect the fundamental forces in international politics that helped to establish periods during which power and institutions are the dominant forces in shaping outcomes (Caporoso, 1992; Ruggie, 1992, 1993).

Norms, ideas, and knowledge may establish the parameters within which power is exercised and institutions are respected. For instance, in the 19th century a dominant worldview based on economic liberalism and reductionist mechanical models of social systems uncoupled from physical systems diffused worldwide and helped to establish a context in which much international behavior is still understood. Now, this collective understanding of world politics subject to state-centric models, within a condition of international anarchy and obeying norms of self-help, may be subject to being modified, replaced, or merely supplemented by a view of interconnected and indeterminate social and physical systems, subject to a norm of stewardship (Ruggie, 1983, 1989, 1993; Kratochwil and Ruggie, 1986; P. Haas, 1992). Although such beliefs are not easily observed or measured, their existence may be inferred from patterns of behavior that reflect them (Wendt, 1987, 1992).

Because the extant theoretical literature is inspired by different ontological commitments, each body of thought addresses only one way of explaining regimes. Each is confined by the choice of actors and mechanisms that it deems appropriate for pursuing its research program within the boundaries of its historical period of experience and inquiry. Neorealist authors, for instance, primarily restrict themselves to studies of the post-Westphalian system, focusing on interstate relations grounded on efforts to promote national preferences, as constrained by the international distribution of material capabilities. They see a world of states endowed with disparate power capabilities that deploy their resources in order to maximize the preferences specified in their utility functions, and, in cases where joint gains are possible, to maximize their relative gains over others (Krasner, 1976; Gilpin, 1981; Grieco, 1990). Since the 1970s, most North American neorealists have self-consciously applied a positivist and mechanistic approach to explaining regimes, out of a belief that patterns of human behavior obey mechanical laws. Consequently, neorealists neglect the influence of non-state actors and of the potential for international influence based on non-material factors.

Institutionalists have focused on the broad institutional factors that may influence states and other international actors in their ability to negotiate joint outcomes that are mutually beneficial (Young, 1989b; Keohane, 1989; Ostrom, 1990; Haas, Keohane, and Levy, 1993). Such studies focus on the context within which regimes emerge and persist, including such factors as norms, and organizational rules and practices that prescribe behavioral rules, constrain activity, and shape expectations (Keohane, 1989, ch. 1). These studies have been largely confined to the post World War II period, and presume the existence of mutual interests. However, they seldom address the origins of such interests or their accuracy.

Cognitivists, in turn, have focused on the role of prevailing forms of reason by which actors identify their preferences, and the available choices facing them (E. Haas, 1980, 1990; Nye, 1987; P. Haas, 1989, 1990, 1992; Adler and Haas, 1992). New regime patterns may result from new information and as a consequence of self-reflection by various actors. Cognitivists treat actors as reflective organisms, rather than as inert matter that obeys universally applicable and unchanging mechanical laws, as neorealists and institutionalists treat them. Consequently, dynamic and autopoietic models are seen as more applicable for capturing regime dynamics and patterns of human behavior over time (Maturana and Varela, 1980). Cognitivists share with institutionalists a concern with norms and beliefs that may shape behavior. However, unlike the institutionalists, who take such factors as given and tend to focus on formal organizations and rules through which such norms are expressed, cognitivists investigate the origins of such beliefs and the dynamics by which they persist and change. More sensitive to historical context than the other two traditions, which aspire to offering universal theoretical propositions, most cognitivist studies of epistemic communities, for instance, have been limited to the period since the Industrial Revolution during which the authoritative form of policy-relevant understanding that policymakers accept has stressed the role of scientific study, and has been articulated and disseminated by experts and professionals.

I argue that the cognitivist approach has the most to offer because of its explicit focus on the actors' perceptions and interpretations, although it also falls prey to the need to consider such traditional factors as the distribution of power. No school yet has a monopoly on explanation. Full explanations of events require a judicious selection from each while we await the development of a meta-framework or meta-theory in which the contributions of each may be incorporated. Thus, an analytically satisfying explanation of responses to environmental threats must borrow from a variety of existing theories, while striving to establish the relevant domain of each (Rosenau, 1990).

Sophisticated approaches to explaining environmental regime patterns are called for because most environmental problems contain significant obstacles to cooperation (Ruggie, 1972; Wijkman, 1982). It is unclear what property rights would even mean with regard to common property resources, which account for 59 percent of all international environmental regimes and 67 percent of all environmental regimes established since 1972 (Haas with Sundgren, 1993) for, "even when particular rights (such as to harvest particular species) are unitized, quantified, and salable, the resource system is still likely to be owned in common rather than individually" (Ostrom, 1990). Thus regimes must be based on coordinated environmental regulations. But by the 1970s, when serious efforts for international environmental protection began, the political problem involved coordinating discordant policies, instruments, and policy philosophies between countries. Because most environmental problems are perceived by leaders to embody conflicting interests, rather than common interests requiring coordination, they are "hard" problems to solve. Regimes are unlikely to emerge spontaneously; they must be negotiated by different users of the threatened resource. Theorists from different traditions of international relations have differing views of how this is likely to occur.

Regime patterns

Most regime analysis has been broken down into the three convenient, discrete categories of regime creation, persistence, and transformation. Underlying these different categories are singular regime patterns or styles of collective management and lesson-drawing associated with regime creation, persistence, and change. Particularly for environmental issues, it is often more reasonable to see these three categories as part of a broader pattern, or as part of a dynamic path (or vector) of cooperation in which nation states accumulate and assimilate rapidly evolving information in an effort collectively to manage a shared problem marked by disagreements over preferences. In this formulation, a major concern for regime analysts is the extent to which participants actually modify their behavior in line with regime obligations. This element, which Oran Young terms "effectiveness", is largely neglected by most neorealists and institutionalists (Rittberger, 1990; Young, 1993).

Different schools of thought describe and analyze discrete patterns. Although much analysis is devoted to explaining specific events, such analysis is grounded in broader research programs aimed at explaining recurrent patterns of behavior. While individual analysts often focus on one feature or characteristic of the pattern, each school of thought ties the features together into different, yet distinct syndromes or patterns of regime characteristics. Analysts typically explain the variation in each characteristic in terms of their tradition's preferred independent variable, be it the distribution of power, state interests, institutional features, consensual knowledge, or involvement of epistemic communities. Thus, for each school of thought, discrete patterns exist of covarying regime features.

Each regime pattern includes a characteristic set of features. These include the political process by which it is created and maintained, the regime's substance, compliance effects on participating countries (effectiveness), and institutional learning.

Regimes are developed, maintained, and changed through a political process, which may be based on state leadership or on institutional bargaining. A regime's substance relates to the types of policies that are collectively endorsed. In turn this has two dimensions: scope and strength. Many environmental regimes vary in the rules' scope, from controlling discrete substances to entire uses of a shared resource. Regimes also vary in terms of the strength of their rules – the stringency of the demands on states' to comply. These may vary from weak, in the case of largely exhortatory regimes, to very strong, in the case of regimes where the use of specific substances is banned. Compromises between scope and strength can be easily imagined. Regime substance also varies in terms of the actual policy instruments that governments choose collectively to endorse.

In turn, each pattern entails a different set of compliance effects on participating countries. Schematically these effects can be analyzed for activist countries, whose environmental policies are initially more advanced than other countries (leaders), and for countries with overall weaker efforts (laggards).

Each pattern also has an attendant style of institutional learning, which pertains to the way in which and extent to which participating countries modify the regime in light of new information. In the context of regimes, as I use it here, "learning" is a political process through which collective behavior is modified in light of new collective understanding (see Breslauer and Tetlock, 1991, for a fuller study of learning). It is an international process that can influence collective behavior that is unrelated to the more commonly studied distribution of material sources of influence. For analytic purposes, to better understand the role of learning in shaping regime patterns, a major independent variable is new information, a major intervening variable is the mode of information processing at the state level, and the dependent variable is the regime pattern.

It is analytically important to distinguish three discrete dimensions of institutional learning. First is the extent of learning. Two types of learning are possible along this dimension. States may modify policies in a discrete area of activity, or they may come to link two areas of activity that had previously been managed independently. Because environmental issues interact with so many other international issues and regimes, investigating the linkage element is important for understanding the conditions under which more holistic and comprehensive environmental and other international policy choices are reached.

This distinction is not the same as a second dimension, which refers to the type of learning that may occur. Recent students of institutional learning have distinguished between whether simple lessons are drawn or complex ones; whether new styles of information processing are applied to existing puzzles.[5] Simple learning (adaptation) may be best measured by whether institutions develop new organizational tasks following the acquisition of new information. Complex learning (learning) may best be measured by the number of references to necessary measures undertaken in other associated areas when states are seeking to establish regime rules within a given domain.

Thirdly, learning may occur in a variety of ways. Institutional adaptation to environmental challenges need not be cognitive (Heclo, 1974; P. Haas, 1990, pp. 58–63; Rose, 1991). A dominant actor may compel other states to accept its preferred policies, while using new information as a justification. Policy change may occur by states emulating or imitating successful public policies adopted elsewhere. No interaction is required in this form. Learning may also occur through an infection model, where one state's policies are adopted elsewhere following the exchange of information and experience among regime participants. The system-wide replacement of one set of bureaucratic actors endowed with a dominant policy paradigm by another may have a similar effect. Learning may also be cognitive, as policymakers and others jointly reflect on their experiences and modify their means and/or ends. Linkages between issues may be forged based on tactical, fragmented, or substantive connections. Tactical and fragmented linkages are likely to persist so long as they serve the short-term political needs of the coalition for which the linkages are useful. Substantive linkages, on the other hand, will probably persist until the scientific basis for the connection is rejected (E. Haas, 1980).

Three master variables are typically invoked by major schools of thought to explain regime patterns. Regime patterns are generally understood analytically in terms of the systemic distribution of material power resources, the distribution of state interests (or preferences), and knowledge (Krasner, 1982; Young, 1993). To some extent an excessively dry distinction is drawn between power and knowledge. The control of knowledge and meaning is surely an important power resource (Cox, 1987). Still, most neorealists and marxist-informed scholars focus on material capabilities as the major source of power and influence. These variables reflect a kaleidoscope of forces that may influence regime patterns and their dynamics; different regime patterns result from different configurations of forces. Comparative studies of environmental regimes have demonstrated that it is impossible to explain regime dynamics in terms of any single variable (Osherenko and Young, 1993; the Tubingen project, P. Haas, 1993).

The distribution of power is the major variable for most international regime analysts, including analysis by realists, neorealists, Marxists, and dependency theorists, and is mechanically invoked to identify correlates of regime patterns. States deploy power resources in pursuit of their preferences. Regime patterns are thus subject to the distribution of power between states. Most realists and neorealists also identify power as a major objective of nation states.

Realists define power in terms of material capabilities. Material capabilities may be concentrated globally, as argued by world systems hegemonic stability theorists, or may be issue-specific. More issue-specific measures of resources that confer influence are often more appropriate for analyzing environmental issues because the basis of power is often unclear when managing pollution. Environmental issue-specific power resources include such factors as controlling enough of a resource that the country possesses a virtual unit veto over collective decisions affecting it, having enough capacity unilaterally to affect the quality of a shared resource, controlling enough trade such that unilateral environmental restrictions would have serious economic consequences for trading partners, and a strong reputation for diplomatic skill and scientific competence.

Purely power-based approaches are limited by their inability to explain how countries are likely to respond to circumstances where state interests are not manifestly clear, or are intimately intertwined with other issues, and where the utility of orthodox policy levers is unclear. In many environmental cases in particular, information about the extent of pollution, its sources, and the necessary means to eliminate it is not sufficiently available or developed to allow a government rationally to formulate a set of objectives.

Institutionalists focus on interests and analyze the context or setting under which cooperation may be valued and pursued by states out of self-interest. Such analysts typically focus on the institutional context in which decisions are taken, seeking to specify features that may promote the possibility of joint gains being realized through regime creation. Actors are generally portrayed as egoistic, rational utility-maximizers, albeit with incomplete information. Their interests are viewed as given and largely invariant. Alternatively, analysts may take actors' statements of their preferences at face value as accurate depictions of their objectives. Knowledge is generally seen to play a minor role, although it can be a source from which actors recognize new interests or appreciate a change in institutional context.

Cooperation can also be understood in terms of knowledge. Scholars who stress perceptions, cognitive processes, and interpretive approaches to understanding international relations commonly stress the role of ideas and knowledge in shaping the perceptions, beliefs, expectations, and preferences of major actors (P. Haas, 1992a). Such theorists argue that interests are often unknown or incompletely specified. Consensus about policy-relevant understanding can contribute to shaping regime patterns. Interests are identified subject to consensual knowledge, and the decision to deploy state power is similarly conditioned. Recently, it appears that such explanations have growing utility, as there has been an emergent environmental regime pattern, driven not only by state power, but by the application of scientific understanding about ecological systems to the management of environmental policy issues with which decision-makers are unfamiliar. The role of scientific or expert understanding in international policy coordination is documented for security and economic issues as well as environmental issues (P. Haas, 1992a).

Scientific knowledge may be best operationalized in terms of epistemic communities. Consensual knowledge does not emerge in isolation, but rather is created and spread by transnational networks of specialists. Under conditions of complex interdependence and generalized uncertainty, specialists play a significant role in attenuating such uncertainty for decision-makers. Leaders and politicians are typically in the dark about the sources of pollution, the extent of contamination, the interaction between emissions and water quality, the costs of clean-up, and the likely actions of their neighbors. Such conditions are particularly puzzling in technical issues that pose low-probability but high-risk outcomes, and specific state interests may be hazy.

In such circumstances, perceptions may be false, leaders may lack adequate information for informed choice, and traditional search procedures and policy-making heuristics are impossible. Information is at a premium, and leaders look for those able to provide authoritative advice to attenuate such uncertainty, and either consult them for policy advice and/or delegate responsibility to them. Subsequent discussions and policy debates are then informed and bounded by the advice that leaders receive. International negotiations may then be viewed "as a process for reducing uncertainty" (Winham, 1977, p. 96), as well as a process of deferring to specialists regarded as possessing a reputation for expertise in the domain of concern. Such experts' influence is subject to their ability to avoid widespread internal disagreement, and their influence persists through their ability to consolidate political power through capturing important bureaucratic positions in national administrations, from which they may persuade other decision-makers or usurp control over decision-making.

In environmental issues, many of these experts have been members of an ecological epistemic community. Epistemic communities are networks of knowledge-based communities with an authoritative claim to policy-relevant knowledge within their domain of expertise (Haas, 1992a). Their members share knowledge about the causation of social or physical phenomena in an area for which they have a reputation for competence, and a common set of normative beliefs about what actions will benefit human welfare in such a domain. In particular, they are a group of professionals, often from a number of different disciplines, who share the following set of characteristics:

(1) Shared consummatory values or principled beliefs. Such beliefs provide a value-based rationale for social action of the members of the community.

(2) Shared causal beliefs or professional judgment. Such beliefs provide analytic reasons and explanations of behavior,

offering causal explanations for the multiple linkages between possible policy actions and desired outcomes.
(3) Common notions of validity: intersubjective, internally defined criteria for validating knowledge.
(4) A common policy enterprise: a set of practices associated with a central set of problems that have to be tackled, presumably out of a conviction that human welfare will be enhanced as a consequence.

Such characteristics may be identified through interviews and studies of specialized publications of technical advisors before their entry into policy-making.

Members of epistemic communities involved in environmental regimes have subscribed to holistic ecological beliefs about the need for policy coordination subject to ecosystemic laws. Thus, they promote international environmental regimes that are grounded on policies that offer coherent plans for the management of entire ecosystems that are sensitive to interactions between environmental media (such as air and water), sources of pollution, and contending uses of the common property resource, rather than being limited to more traditional policies for managing discrete activities or physical resources spaces within fairly short-term time horizons.

Neorealism and "follow the leader"

Neorealists such as Kenneth Waltz, Robert Gilpin, Joseph Grieco, and David Lake (Waltz, 1979; Gilpin, 1981; Lake, 1988; Grieco, 1990) argue that, in the absence of centralized authority, collective behavior is shaped by the strongest country. Cooperation and effective management are likely to emerge only from the concentration or balance of international power, rather than from the emergence of technical concerns. In the absence of compulsion to coordinate their efforts, governments act principally to insulate their domestic sphere of policy-making, thereby acting to reduce the influence of any other groups on their actions (i.e. international organizations, other governments, or multinational corporations), as well as eliminating any forms of international obligations they may accept in order to protect the environment. To the extent that non-state actors are considered, they are generally believed to have little long-term influence on how such state patterns of action are developed. When cooperation occurs, it is led by a hegemon, and predominantly reflects the hegemon's concerns.

Neorealists predict that regimes are likely to emerge only when a systemic concentration of material power resources exists. Regimes will persist so long as such a power concentration exists; regimes will decline with the diffusion of international power. Such authors argue that environmental regimes will be created by a dominant country that leads other countries to accept a regime that it prefers. The regime is created by the strongest party and other countries are compelled by that country to join and comply. The regime persists as others emulate the dominant country, or are compelled by the dominant country to coordinate their policies. The regime persists until the hegemon's control over tangible resources declines, after which the regime collapses. The actual substance of the regime is a projection of the dominant country's particular preferences. Its preferences often vary, from broad and inchoate foreign policy (such as funneling assistance to one's allies or opening up new diplomatic channels) to efforts to get other countries to conform with the dominant country's past policy experience in order to create a level playing field.

The regime may be either strongly or weakly regulatory, depending upon the dominant country's prior domestic experience. For instance, US–Mexican environmental arrangements impose stronger US regulatory standards on the less environmentally rigorous Mexicans, whereas the US–Canadian acid rain regime is primarily a joint research operation, owing to US preferences that are laxer than Canada's.

The level of regime effectiveness will depend upon whether the dominant party's environmental policies are more or less stringent than those of other countries. In either case, the dominant party presses smaller countries to modify their policies to accommodate its preferences. Politically weaker laggard countries have to improve their policies. Politically weaker countries with initially more stringent measures, however, may be less prone to abandon them and to approach a lower hegemonic preference because of established domestic routines and expectations among domestic groups that the more stringent standards have fostered. Other countries' compliance varies according to the dominant party's willingness to supervise and compel others to enforce the regime rules, because of the constant temptation to defect and the need for a centralized authority to oversee arrangements.

Learning is likely to be fairly limited because foreign policy makers in the dominant country tend to be more concerned with political or economic considerations than technical ones. Learning will be simple rather than complex. The only policy and linkage learning likely to occur involves modifying the dominant country's security and economic objectives in light of technical lessons about the environment that may inhibit the pursuit of existing foreign policy objectives. Other countries may be forced to accept the policies of the dominant country, or they may learn by copying policies in the hegemon; for instance many US Environmental Protection Agency regulations are applied elsewhere in the world (Brickman, Jasanoff, and Ilgen, 1985). Environmental issues are likely to be linked only tactically to other issues, owing to the absence of serious input from ecological scientists to negotiations and the reluctance of states to accept policies that may circumscribe national autonomy or sovereignty or that may be expensive to implement.

US leadership has been key in shaping global atmospheric regimes. The United States exercised significant influence in negotiating the 1992 climate change treaty, and successfully pressured the European Community to water down the treaty's strength to reflect the relatively weaker existing US domestic energy conservation and carbon dioxide emission policies. Similarly, the relatively weak 1985 Vienna Convention for the Protection of the Stratospheric Ozone Layer, which established the stratospheric ozone protection regime, was also strongly shaped by US leadership and opposition to European efforts to control CFC production (Benedick, 1991; P. Haas 1992b).

Institutionalism and bargaining patterns

Contractual institutionalists who are informed by social choice approaches focus on bargaining structures through which regimes are created and maintained. Such authors as Robert Axelrod, Robert Keohane, Elinor Ostrom, Arild Underdal, and Oran Young exemplify this tradition (Underdal, 1982; Keohane, 1984, 1989; Keohane and Axelrod, 1986; Young, 1989a, b, 1993; Ostrom, 1990). They assume a common area of interests, and seek to specify institutional factors that may encourage actors to overcome their reluctance to cooperate. Individuals are deemed to be constructive, information-seeking actors. The policy question is how to provide them with sufficient incentives – of which information is one – to ensure they produce outcomes beneficial to the international community, such as preserving the environment. Power is not as important an explanation as is the opportunity for finding joint gains from cooperation. States' recognition of their preferences is essential for successfully applying bargaining techniques, as well as understanding states' behavior in collective negotiations.

Institutionalists believe that regime-creation efforts would be further inhibited when a large number of parties is involved in environmental protection. For instance, large numbers of parties would make regime creation more difficult, and increase the likelihood of very weak and transitory regimes. Conversely, smaller numbers would increase the possibility that institutional bargaining could lead to more stringent and durable regimes (Olson, 1965; Baumol, 1971).

Institutionalists expect to find negotiated regimes whose substance merely reflects the measures tolerable to the least enthusiastic party; in essence, the least common denominator (LCD). Arild Underdal has formulated this behavioral pattern as the "law of the least ambitious program" (Underdal, 1982; Saetevik, 1988). Consequently, collective measures are often far too diffuse and weak significantly to improve environmental quality. Such behavioral patterns are widely evident in the management of international fisheries, and obtained in collective efforts to protect the North Sea and Baltic from pollution until 1987.

LCD regimes are largely formalizations of the least stringent existing national efforts. Such regimes would typically lack serious compliance measures, and regulatory standards would tend to be extremely weak. In regions where countries have no or weak standards, the regime will be correspondingly modest. If states have stronger standards, the weakest one will serve as the regime norm. Since national obligations are meager, compliance is a relatively minor matter. As with the "follow the leader" pattern, backsliding by states with stronger measures is unlikely owing to domestic conditions. Some simple emulatory policy learning may be possible, but more sophisticated institutional learning is unlikely because governments are driven by experience and a reluctance to accept new obligations, and joint decisions reflect the views of the least enthusiastic party.

Some alternatives to the LCD option exist. Stronger regime patterns are possible if negotiations occur within a setting of institutional bargaining or if certain institutional design factors obtain. Oran Young characterizes institutional bargaining as the setting in which regimes are created and maintained through bargaining between several distinct types of actors, including states and NGOs, in an organizational context and subject to uncertainty about the costs and benefits of cooperation (Young, 1989a, 1993). While actors are seeking to obtain their own preferences, they may not be fully certain what they are. In such circumstances, Young expects that actors will have only a weak regard for distributional effects.

In institutional bargaining, leadership can come from a country, entrepreneurial individual diplomats, or non-state actors, including international organizations, nongovernmental organizations, or epistemic communities. Such a leader can help identify compromises from which everyone else may benefit. With the use of such techniques as stressing uncertainty, monitoring, iterated games, promoting equity, and integrative bargaining over debate on distributive and efficiency issues, and the introduction of such "selective incentives" as side payments, political pressure, education, and the like, designers may create and maintain regimes through bargaining that exceed the LCD model.

Robert Axelrod, Robert Keohane, Elinor Ostrom, and Oran Young identify other institutional factors by which negotiated regimes may exceed the limited scope of LCD regimes (Keohane and Axelrod, 1986; Ostrom, 1990; Kremenyuk, 1991). They observe that stronger long-lasting regimes are possible when it is easy to monitor and verify actors' compliance with major behavioral obligations, the numbers of participants are relatively small, actors are engaged in iterated games, and actors are encouraged to consider the long-term effects of their actions (the shadow of the future). Institutionally created regimes may persist if participants come to appreciate the value provided by the regime, and realize that continued cooperation is preferable to a relapse into policy disorder. Regimes established by a hegemon may also persist past hegemonic decline for institutional reasons, as Robert Keohane argues with regard to international economic regimes (Keohane, 1984).

Hegemonically inherited regimes may be regulatory in form if they were originally designed with regulatory standards. Most of the regimes with which institutionalists have been concerned were established under the hegemonic auspices of the United States. While such regimes as GATT and the international monetary regime have limped on past the decline of US hegemony, their regulatory form was the result of initial US shaping of the regime. Under more recent conditions of interdependency without hegemony, regulatory efforts have been fewer and harder to obtain: GATT had serious problems in concluding the Uruguay Round, regulatory trade arrangements have been concluded regionally where strong disparities of power and leverage continue to obtain, the effort to regulate international commodity trade has largely died (see Chapter 3 in this volume by Hveem) and the International Energy Agency countries deliberately avoided invoking their regulatory commitments in 1979 out of well-founded fears that they may have failed and thus undermined any legitimacy that the consumers' oil regime commanded.

Environmental regimes concluded in the aftermath of hegemony may aspire to regulatory content, but the regulations are unlikely to exceed LCD levels initially because countries tend to disagree profoundly about appropriate regulatory standards for environmental protection. Regimes are likely to be designed to encourage the provision of information about the quality of the environment (monitoring) and about other countries' pollution control activities, to administer pollution control facilities, or to pay clean-up costs from a joint insurance fund. These are international functions that are generally regarded as desirable in the environmental realm, both on their own merits and because they backstop a regulatory regime by quickly alerting parties to defections. (The general economic or social functions that these activities fulfill can be found in Keohane, 1982, 1984; Keohane and Axelrod, 1986).

Institutional bargaining may contribute to movement away from the LCD over time, subject to domestic-level pressures. As national environmental pressures mount, governments are forced to try to persuade their neighbors to adopt stronger measures as well, creating a ratcheting element in the LCD process. Important domestic pressures include the division of powers between the federal and state levels, legal traditions, administrative organization and expertise, relations between the judiciary and administration, and a country's research system and its input into public policy (Brickman, Jasanoff, and Ilgen 1985; Hoberg, forthcoming).

Regimes resulting from bargaining will demand stronger compliance from laggards than from leaders. Because the regime will probably end up with measures that are weaker than in the strongest country, little accommodation is required by the leader. But laggard countries will have to beef up their measures to comply with the regime. Leaders may even have their efforts inhibited or retarded by other countries, which would urge them to go slowly in their adoption of more rigorous standards that could introduce incompatibilities between national systems that they are trying to harmonize. For instance, Sweden's efforts to reduce sulphur dioxide emissions from autos were slowed by up to two years by the EC's reluctance to adopt similar measures for the Community (Boehmer-Christiansen, 1984).

Environmental regimes that provide incentives for states to participate are likely to be more effective than ones that do not. Major factors that encourage state compliance include regime features that create a stable bargaining environment, so that ongoing negotiations are possible and future expectations of rewards are created; enhancing national concern, so governments are held accountable by their populations for complying with international obligations; and offering improvements in state capacity so that states are rewarded for their participation and find it easier to comply with their obligations (Haas, Keohane, and Levy, 1993).

Learning in institutional bargaining is possible. New policies may be identified and adopted, and some issue linkage is also possible. Because actors are engaged largely in integrative bargaining involving exploratory forays to determine the exact shape of the bargaining Pareto frontier, new scientific findings and consensual knowledge may lead actors to link issues substantively in a regime. Many processes of learning are possible within international institutions: through demonstration effects laggard countries may gradually come to emulate stronger policies applied elsewhere; and information may be exchanged by experts leading environment ministers to adopt new measures. While policies may be imitated by other countries, most countries will remain strongly conditioned by the fear of unreciprocated policies and hence fail to adopt new policies that would threaten competitiveness.

Such an approach may have significant value for understanding European environmental negotiations, where many countries have already adopted domestic environmental measures and there are clear reasons for harmonizing national efforts. It is difficult to apply institutional insights to issues where countries with strong domestic environmental protection measures are reluctant to engage in meaningful international discussions, such as the United States during the 1980s.

Limits exist for the applicability of institutional bargaining techniques. If issues are not widely regarded as generating collective outcomes for all, such techniques are unlikely to be effective. Even if actors share common aversions (an assurance game), there will be eventual distributional squabbles – perhaps in a second game – which, if actors rationally anticipate, means that they will even be unwilling to engage in constructive bargaining to resolve the first, easier problem (Bates, 1988; Ostrom, 1990, pp. 42–3).

Cognitivism and modified "follow the leader"

A focus on epistemic communities suggests that the patterns predicted by neorealists and institutionalists require modifications. Cognitivists stress that the international system is often far more indeterminate than assumed by scholars from other traditions. Thus, uncertainty is pervasive and states' interests are often unclear. In such circumstances, epistemic communities may significantly influence the patterns that regimes assume.

Epistemic communities are likely to be found in substantive issues where scientific disciplines have been applied to policy-oriented work and in countries with well-established institutional capacities for administration and science and technology. Only governments with such capacities would have need for the technical skills that epistemic community members command, and such professionals would be attracted to governmental service only when they believe that their policy enterprise can be advanced. Crises or widely publicized shocks are probably necessary precipitants of environmental regime creation, but crises alone are insufficient to be able to explain how or which collective responses to a perceived joint problem are likely to develop.

Under conditions of uncertainty, when international power is concentrated in one state, and when epistemic communities have successfully consolidated influence in the dominant state, then the "follow the leader" pattern may be modified in light of the policy beliefs of the epistemic community. The regime would still be created through the intercession of the hegemon, but its substance would reflect epistemic consensus. In other respects this pattern would be similar to "follow the leader": other countries' behavior remain subject to the influence of the hegemon. The regime's persistence would still covary with hegemonic tenure, unless the hegemon promoted the involvement of epistemic community members in other governments, in which case the regime would be likely to continue through the epistemically informed bargaining pattern discussed in the next section. Environmental regimes created under modified hegemonic leadership are likely to be more comprehensive in scope than straight hegemonic ones, owing to the shaping influence of the ecological epistemic community. Substantive institutional learning is possible as policies and linkages can be informed by the ecological insights of the epistemic community. Such learning may occur through persuasion and bureaucratic clout exercised by members of the epistemic community in countries where they have consolidated their bureaucratic influence, and by emulation and other patterns in other countries. The development and modification of the international regime for stratospheric ozone protection since 1985 fit this pattern (P. Haas, 1992).

Cognitivism and epistemically informed bargaining

Cognitivists argue that when epistemic communities are widely spread, even in the absence of leadership by a strong state, environmentally effective regimes are possible. Environmental regimes in this instance emerge through institutional bargaining, as described by institutionalists. Regimes are most likely to be created following widely publicized environmental disasters that mobilize public and experts' demands for governmental action. Regime negotiation and maintenance would be characterized by conference diplomacy, with many countries seeking to resolve shared problems subject to the technical advice that they receive from their own experts, NGOs, transnational scientific networks, and international organizations. Non-state actors play an important role.

As epistemic communities obtain and consolidate influence in different governments, national preferences and policies would come to reflect the epistemic beliefs. The secretariats of international organizations can play a key role in such patterns as sources of information and new policy ideas, as well as buffering political differences between the parties. Epistemic communities have often lodged themselves in international organizations as well, in particular the United Nations Environment Program.

The negotiated regime would then reflect the causal and principled beliefs of the epistemic community. National positions would vary according to the extent of penetration by epistemic communities, or the sensitivity of policies in that country to policies in a country already influenced by the epistemic community. In most cases this would make epistemic environmental regimes more stringent and comprehensive than other forms of environmental regimes, owing to the more sophisticated vision of ecological problems that ecological epistemic communities hold. Regimes will be regulatory. Regimes will persist until the epistemic community's shared body of knowledge collapses. Both leaders and laggards might modify their policies in light of the new regime as a bandwagoning process develops, leading to gradual, progressively increasing changes in national policies to accommodate evolving scientific understanding about how ecosystems work. As with other patterns, anticipations of material rewards from the regime (i.e. capacity-building provisions) would also encourage states to comply with the regime.

Learning would reflect lessons imparted by the epistemic community. Policies and linkages may be quite sophisticated, reflecting the quality of its beliefs. The extent to which such lessons are accepted and converted into new policies in different countries, as well as regime compliance, are subject to the ability of members of the epistemic community to occupy key bureaucratic slots and to persuade others of their preferred policies. They may encourage governments to undertake new patterns of economic development based on more complex and integrated visions of ecological interactions, organize issues in novel ways, and make decision-makers aware of possibilities for mutual gain from cooperation that they had not previously recognized.

Learning in this context may be quite complex, in the sense that policymakers recognize or appreciate new connections between issues that were previously regarded as distinct. Epistemic communities may lead policymakers to reflect on their objectives and to link issues in novel ways, subject to an ecological understanding of global ecological dynamics and a dawning recognition of extensive interplay between environmental protection and other state concerns. As such actors intercede in policy-making, they may change national attitudes toward environmental protection, thereby overcoming the antipathy to institutional creation and international cooperation. Decision-makers would become more likely to link issues based on their substantive connections. New institutions would be created by bargaining and by such groups' gradual insinuation into international secretariats and national bureaucracies, rather than by state leadership.

The epistemic community pattern may well have differential impacts on developed countries (DCs) and less developed countries (LDCs). DCs with greater familiarity and ability to evaluate external advice, will be more likely to defer to transnational scientific advice. Conversely, many LDCs are highly suspicious of technical advice and information from abroad, and will defer only to scientific advice that is provided through domestic channels. The development of indigenous scientific capability reinforces the authority of those scientists providing advice to decision-makers.

Conclusion

These three theoretical approaches to the study of international regimes offer different hypotheses concerning regime patterns under different conditions. Neorealists predict patterns of "follow the leader" under conditions of concentrated systemic power, and much weaker and transitory regimes under other conditions. Institutionalists expect to see LCD regimes in cases with large numbers of actors and where the institutional techniques identified by institutionalist authors are not applied. When they are applied, they expect to see regime patterns that follow the bargaining pattern, regardless of the distribution of power or knowledge.

Cognitivists modify these hypotheses under conditions when epistemic communities are present. With a high concentration of systemic power, cognitivists expect to see modified "follow the leader" patterns, and epistemically informed bargaining patterns under conditions of diffused power.

The next challenge is to apply empirical studies to such a conceptual framework. Tentative conclusions suggest that the real world consists of a hybrid of these different predicted patterns. For instance, the Mediterranean Action Plan falls within the domains of these three traditions: between 1970 and 1975 regional power was concentrated; from 1976 to 1980 regional concentration of power overlapped with an epistemic community; and since 1980 the epistemic community has existed in the absence of significant concentration of capabilities (P. Haas, 1990). It would be a mistake to consider the special case of a parsimonious theory that successfully explains one period or set of regime features as justification for generalizing that parsimonious theories are more useful than more complex ones (Ostrom, 1990). More complex theories are necessary to explain the dynamic evolution of environmental regimes that may demonstrate different patterns at different points in time.

Acknowledgements

I am grateful to Helge Hveem, Robert O. Keohane, and Arild Underdal for their comments on this essay, which draws from a broader theoretical and empirical argument presented in "Epistemic Communities and the Dynamics of International Environmental Cooperation" in Volker Rittberger, ed. *Beyond Anarchy: International Cooperation and Regimes* (New York: Oxford University Press, forthcoming).

Notes

1 See Argyris and Schon (1978), Nye (1987), E. Haas (1990), P. Haas (1990, pp. 58-63, Breslauer and Tetlock (1991). Argyris and Schon speak of single and double loop learning, Nye of simple and complex learning, E. Haas of adaptation and learning, but the distinction is roughly equivalent in all usages.

References

Adler, Emanuel, and Peter M. Haas (1992) "Epistemic Communities, International Cooperation and World Order: Creating a Reflective Research Program," *International Organization*, vol. 46, no. 1 (Winter), pp. 367–90.

Argyris, Chris, and Donald A. Schon (1978) *Organizational Learning* (Reading, Mass: Addison-Wesley).

Bates, Robert (1988) "Contra Contractarianism", *Politics and Society,* vol. 16, pp. 387–401.

Baumol, William J. (1971) *Environmental Protection, International Spillovers, and Trade* (Uppsala: Almqvist & Wiksel).

Benedick, Richard (1991) *Ozone Diplomacy* (Cambridge, Mass.: Harvard University Press.

Boehmer-Christiansen, Sonia (1984) "Marine Pollution Control in Europe," *Marine Policy,* vol. 8, no. 1 (January), pp. 44–55.

Breslauer, George W., and Philip E. Tetlock, eds (1991) *Learning in U.S. and Soviet Foreign Policy* (Boulder, Colo.: Westview Press).

Brickman, Ronald, Sheila Jasanoff, and Thomas Ilgen (1985) *Controlling Chemicals. The Politics of Regulation in Europe and the United States* (Ithaca, NY: Cornell University Press).

Caporoso, James A. (1992) "International Relations Theory and Multilateralism," *International Organization,* vol. 46, no. 3 (Summer), pp. 599–632.

Cox, Robert (1987) *Production, Power, and World Order* (New York: Columbia University Press).

Gilpin, Robert (1981) *War and Change in World Politics* (Cambridge: Cambridge University Press).

Grieco, Joseph M. (1990) *Cooperation Among Nations* (Ithaca, NY: Cornell University Press).

Haas, Ernst B. (1980) "Why Collaborate? Issue-Linkage and International Regimes," *World Politics,* vol. 32, no. 3 (April), pp. 357–405.

Haas, Ernst B. (1990) *When Knowledge is Power* (Berkeley: University of California Press).

Haas, Peter M. (1989) "Do Regimes Matter? Epistemic Communities and Mediterranean Pollution Control," *International Organization,* vol. 43, no. 3 (Summer), pp. 377–404.

Haas, Peter M. (1990) *Saving the Mediterranean. The Politics of International Environmental Cooperation* (New York: Columbia University Press).

Haas, Peter M., ed (1992a) *Knowledge, Power and International Policy Coordination. A special issue of International Organization,* vol. 46, no. 1 (Winter).

Haas, Peter M. (1992b) "Banning Chlorofluorocarbons," *International Organization,* vol. 46, no. 1 (Winter), pp. 187–224.

Haas, Peter M. (1992c) "From Theory to Practice: Ecological Ideas and

Development Policy," Paper No. 92–2, Working Papers Series, Harvard University Center for International Affairs.

Haas, Peter M., with Jan Sundgren (1993) "Evolving International Environmental Law and Changing Practices of National Sovereignty," in Nazli Choucri, eds (1993) *Global Accord: Environmental Challenges and International Response*s (Cambridge, Mass.: MIT Press).

Haas, Peter M., Robert O. Keohane, and Marc A. Levy, eds (1993) *Institutions for the Earth: Sources of Effective International Environmental Protection* (Cambridge, Mass.: MIT Press).

Heclo, Hugh (1974) *Modern Social Policies in Britain and Sweden* (New Haven, Conn.: Yale University Press).

Hoberg, George (forthcoming) "Governing the Environment: Comparing Policies in Canada and the United States," in Keith Banting and Richard Simeon, eds, *Canada and the United States in a Changing World. Vol 2*

Keohane, Robert O. (1982) "The Demand for International Regimes," in S. Krasner, ed. *International Regimes*, (Ithaca, NY: Cornell University Press), pp. 141–72.

Keohane, Robert O. (1984) *After Hegemony* (Princeton, NJ: Princeton University Press).

Keohane, Robert O. (1989) *International Institutions and State Power* (Boulder, Colo.: Westview Press).

Keohane, Robert O., and Robert Axelrod (1986) "Achieving Cooperation Under Anarchy: Strategies and Institutions," in Kenneth Oye, ed. *Cooperation Under Anarchy* (Princeton, NJ: Princeton University Press), pp. 226–54.

Krasner, Stephen D. (1976) "State Power and the Structure of International Trade," *World Politics*, vol. 28, no. 3 (April).

Krasner, Stephen D. (1982) "Structural Causes and Regime Consequences," in S. D. Krasner, ed., *International Regimes* (Ithaca, NY: Cornell University Press), pp. 1–22.

Kratochwil, Friedrich, and John G. Ruggie (1986) "International Organization: A State of the Art on an Art of the State," *International Organization*, vol. 40, no. 4 (Autumn), pp. 753–76.

Kremenyuk, Viktor A., ed. (1991) *International Negotiation* (San Francisco: Jossey-Bass).

Lake, David (1988) *Power, Protection, and Free Trade: International Sources of U.S. Commercial Strategy, 1887–1939* (Ithaca, NY: Cornell University Press).

Maturana, Humberto R., and Francisco Varela (1980) *Autopoiesis and Cognition: The Realization of the Living* (Dordrecht: Reidel).

Nye, Joseph S. (1987) "Nuclear Learning," *International Organization*, vol. 41, no. 3 (Summer), pp. 371–402.

Olson, Mancur (1965) *The Logic of Collective Action* (Cambridge, Mass.: Harvard University Press).

Osherenko, Gail, and Oran Young, eds (1993) *Politics of International Regime Formation* (Ithaca, NY: Cornell University Press).

Ostrom, Elinor (1990) *Governing the Commons. The Evolution of Institutions for Collective Action* (Cambridge: Cambridge University Press).

Rittberger, Volker, ed. (1990) *International Regimes in East–West Politics* (London: Pinter Publishers).

Rose, Richard (1991) "What is Lesson-Drawing?" *Journal of Public Policy*, vol. 11, no. 1, pp. 3–30.

Rosenau, James N. (1990) *Turbulence in World Politics* (Princeton, NJ: Princeton University Press).

Ruggie, John Gerard (1972), "Collective Goods and Future International Collaboration," *American Political Science Review*, vol. 66. pp.

Ruggie, John Gerard (1983) "Continuity and Transformation in the World Polity," *World Politics*, vol. 35 (January), pp. 261–85.

Ruggie, John Gerard (1989) "International Structure and International Transformation," in Ernst-Otto Czempiel and James N. Rosenau, eds, *Global Changes and Theoretical Challenges* (Lexington, Mass.: Lexington Books).

Ruggie, John Gerard (1992) "Multilateralism: The Anatomy of an Institution," *International Organization*, vol. 46, no. 3 (Summer), pp. 561–98.

Ruggie, John Gerard (1993) "Finding Our Feet in Territoriality," *International Organization*, vol. 47, no. 4 (Autumn).

Sætevik, Sunneva (1988) *Environmental Cooperation between the North Sea States* (London: Belhaven Press).

Underdal, Arild (1982) "Causes of Negotiation Failure," *European Journal of Political Research*, vol. 11, pp. 183–95.

Waltz, Kenneth (1979) *Theory of International Politics* (Reading, Mass.: Addison-Wesley).

Wendt, Alexander E. (1987) "The Agent – Structure Problem," *International Organization*, vol. 41 (Summer), pp. 335–70.

Wendt, Alexander E. (1992) "Anarchy is What States Make of It," *International Organization*, vol. 46, no. 2 (Spring), pp. 391–426.

Wijkman, Per Magnus (1982) "Managing the Global Commons," *International Organization*, vol. 36, no. 3, pp. 511–36.

Winham, Gilbert R. (1977) "Negotiation as a Management Process," *World Politics*, vol. 30, no. 1 (October).

Young, Oran R. (1989a) "The Politics of International Regime Creation," *International Organization*, vol. 43, no. 3 (Summer), pp. 349–76.

Young, Oran R. (1989b) *International Cooperation: Building Regimes for Natural Resources and the Environment* (Ithaca, NY: Cornell University Press).

Young, Oran R. (1992) "The Effectiveness of International Institutions: Hard Cases and Critical Variables," in James N. Rosenau and Ernst-Otto Czempiel, eds, *Governance Without Government: Order and Change in World Politics* (Cambridge: Cambridge University Press), pp. 160–94.

Young, Oran R. (1993) "Negotiating an International Climate Regime: Institutional Bargaining for Environmental Governance Systems," in Nazli Choucri, ed., *Global Accord: Environmental Challenges and International Responses* (Cambridge, Mass.: MIT Press).

Interests, Property Rights, and Problems of Cooperation
Failing and facilitating international agreement in commodities

Helge Hveem

The problem

Attempts at collective international management of commodities have for several decades occupied a prominent place on the agenda of international trade negotiations. The purpose of this paper is to try to answer a broad, but – as it seems – very timely question: For what purpose, to what degree and indeed whether at all may international trade in commodities be regulated through some type of international cooperative management?

The issue has remained contentious for most of the post World War II era. Not only have achievements in actual cooperative management been modest. The very issue of how to manage, in particular whether to manage by multilateral institutions, is still a matter of contention. This applies both to raw materials and to industrial goods as witnessed by the failure to implement the Havana Charter's International Trade Organization (ITO), the very late implementation of a much-weakened Integrated Programmes for Commodities (IPC) and the protracted and still not fully completed negotiations in the Uruguay Round which are supposed to lead to the setting up of the World Trade Organization (MTO).

Why is this so? Clearly multilateralism as an idea and ideology is still very alive. In practice, however, it has had very mixed success. The trend of the 1970s and 1980s has been to attempt to spread it into new sectors and issue areas that were previously outside the scope of institutionalized cooperative effort. There has, in other words, been more widening than deepening of attempts to make multilateral arrangements work. The result in many areas has been unproductive, or the effort has been met by serious obstacles of different kinds; commodity trade is one example. At the same time there have been some successes in other arenas. They include one that is a relative newcomer – management of international resources and of global environment problems, the commons.

Is the explanation for the observed variance in "success"[1] found in applying an *issue characteristics* approach, that is: is there something inherent in commodities that makes cooperation more difficult in commodities than in environment protection? Are environmental problems thus relatively more, and commodity problems relatively less, benign? (As we shall see, several aspects of resource management involve both the typical commodity agreement agenda and that of environmental protection.)

Now, there are exceptions to this generally bleak picture for commodities, such as a handful of single-commodity agreements that have periodically functioned comparatively effectively. Some of them, such as coffee and tin, appear to owe their initial relative successes to political factors. Is the explanation thus a realist one? Should the variance in outcome be explained by *structural* approaches, emphasizing the impact of power structures, and the international division of labor? What is the role played by economic factors such as *market cycles*? Is the explanation rather to be found in non-realist, *organizational-processual* or in *idiosyncratic* factors, such as the learning and adaptability of organizations, the design and the timing of efforts to reach negotiating breakthroughs, the presence or not of skilled and reputed entrepreneurs in the process of negotiation, the emergence of consensual knowledge, the role of ideology and/or particular interests in determining actor preferences and negotiation goals, or similar factors?

At a very general level of analysis, all these three (four) perspectives merit our attention. We shall substantiate this assumption a bit further, proceed to reformulate the problem in terms of Property rights, and then link property rights to the state–market dimension. These two dimensions represent the heart of matters on which international commodity politics have centered and which basically have been revolving around the question of distributing both power and wealth, the former as much as the latter (Krasner, 1985). But, as we shall see, the analysis may and should be extended to include the issue of sustainable development that is resource management. Such extension may also under certain conditions increase opportunities for cooperative solutions in commodity trade.

A first stab: historical background

Cooperative multilateral management of commodities has been advocated primarily by those countries that have experienced the most severe effects of cyclical changes in international demand and prices for primary commodities, or whose dependence on export incomes from raw materials has been the greatest. Developing or less developed countries, in other words, have been the natural frontrunners in demanding multilateral regulation ever since the preparations for the Bretton Woods order and the Havana Charter started (Mark and Weston, 1989).

This group of countries, however, had no bargaining power whatsoever at the time. They were thus totally dependent on others leading the way, that is on an implicit coalition with the cross-Atlantic community, mostly of civil servants and economists and mostly American, which had set up a system of close control and Allied coordination of raw materials' use during World War II. The fact that the Havana Charter and the ITO were negotiated at all should be ascribed to this community.

But despite an important cross-Atlantic coalition, which apparently included Keynes, the Havana Charter envisaged only very modest departures from the principle of market non intervention in the individual agreements that were to be negotiatiod. And in the end ITO did not materialize. Consensual knowledge about the virtues of non-market commodity control was not shared by sufficiently many influential people and institutions, and it was outright opposed by free-marketeers. Those who wanted to see some carry-over from World War II experiences with commodity control schemes were sufficiently strong to carry the general idea through the negotiating stages, but far from strong enough to prevent the final draft Charter from being watered down and much less *dirigiste* than their original design wanted it. It was finally turned down by the US Congress under the influence of free-marketeers. The hegemonic state thus appeared split in two ideology or policy communities, those of interventionists and free-marketeers, the latter being the stronger. We may refer to them as *redistributive* and *competitive* regulators. Although the latter dominated the scene, we find both active throughout the years that follow Havana.

The existence of an alternative and much stronger pole of consensual knowledge thus prevented the redistributive regulation scheme from being implemented. Indirectly, however, the Charter produced some visible results. Chapter VI anticipated the establishment of international commodity agreements (ICAs). Such agreements were to be set up on an ad hoc basis, monitored under the Economic and Social Council of the UN, and they were recognized by the GATT without the organization taking any active part in their evolution. The ICAs that were formed from the 1950s on – in coffee, sugar, wheat, and tin in particular – were living a life outside the collective system of the UN family until events in the 1970s brought them into the mainstream as part of the negotiations over a New International Economic Order. Whereas GATT did recognize (in an addition to Chapter IV) the need for measures to attain "stable, equitable and remunerative prices" for primary commodities in 1965, it was the active work of the UNCTAD Secretariat from 1974 on, much in the spirit of its first Secretary General, Raúl Prebisch, that gave serious attention to multilateral commodity management.

A brief historical overview of the post World War II period offers a first cut into the empirical question of what causes the success and the failure of commodity agreements. This period may be divided into four relatively distinct sub-periods:

(1) *Geopolitical accommodation.* This sub-period ended around the beginning of the 1960s. It was characterized by the type of "middleground" position that was not regulatory enough for exporting developing countries and a little too much regulatory for corporate business interests, respectively, but that was mainly a result of geopolitical considerations in the hegemonic state. It appeared to be cast in the spirit of the kind of compromise that Polanyi partly advocated, partly predicted in *The Great Transformation*[2].

The compromise allowed for specific redistributive regulation in order to meet foreign policy goals associated with containment and stabilization of potentially unstable regimes in the South without challenging the position of private property rights carried by vested business interests in mines and plantations. In minerals perceived to be of particular strategic interest for the hegemon, the regulation ideology was interventionist (Paley Commission, 1952).

This compromising produced several ICAs, including the International Coffee Agreement, which over a long period offered Latin American producing and exporting countries relatively stable and sometimes above-market prices in exchange for political stability and close support of Western foreign policy positions. Since those states that benefited from the ICAs had little or no bargaining power, it is probably correct to assume that whatever benefits they produced for the South were a gift, a donation from the hegemonic state and its allies[3].

(2) *From clientelism to mobilization.* This sub-period originated in the critique of North–South exchange patterns associated with the

Prebisch/Singer analysis of terms of trade and the more radical unequal exchange theories (Prebisch, 1949; Singer, 1950; Emmanuel, 1972). But mobilization of Southern demands was also a function of decolonization and its companion, rising national consciousness in the former colonial, commodity-exporting countries.

Whereas these countries during the first sub-period obtained an element of more "stable and remunerative" prices in some commodities as a donation given them for mostly geopolitical reasons, this second sub-period represented a manifestation of demands for redistributive regulation as a right held by the South. Collective clientelism, which is another appropriate term for the first sub-period, partially gave ground to manifestations of collective property as a goal, that is, collective demands by actors in the South for greater control over sources of wealth located in territory under their formal juridisction. Donation and clientelism gave ground to politicization.

The sub-period was, however, a time of competing tendencies. It started in the spirit of Kennedy's Alliance for Progress and the EEC's Yaounde Agreement (later Lomé Convention), which were both initiated with partly clientelist, partly more genuinely cooperative motives (Ravenhill, 1985). It led to increasing development assistance and culminated in the fulfillment of demands for collective property rights embodied in price actions by the Organization of Petroleum-Exporting Countries (OPEC). OPEC's achievement became a model of sorts and triggered an instant proliferation of similar attempts to form cartels in a number of commodities (Hveem, 1978). But clientelism never disappeared.

(3) *Complex bargaining*. Complex bargaining on a multi-commodity regime. Backed by OPEC's obvious success and assisted by particular circumstances[4], the South launched an initiative through the non-aligned movement. The initiative to set up a New International Economic Order (NIEO) was channeled into the UN system and resulted *inter alia* in negotiations on an Integrated Programme of Commodities. The UNCTAD IV conference in Nairobi in 1976 rep-

resented a peak for these efforts, setting off a process that turned out to be both complex and timeconsuming. The main redistributive instruments were to be price stabilization measures, mainly buffer stocks to be partly financed through a common fund but separately operated in a series of individual commodity agreements. The prime target for Southern demands was price instability and what was perceived as a tendency to deterioriation in the terms of trade of commodity-exporting less developed countries and resultant loss of income (Hveem, 1977; Finlayson and Zacher, 1988). A second target of the IPC was to support structural diversification in exporting LDCs. Some countries of the South even demanded that a system of indexation be introduced whereby prices of export commodity products would be set as a function (certain percentage) of prices of manufactured products imported to the South.

The negotiating process had in it strong elements of confrontation and straightforward conflict of interest (Hveem, 1977; Rothstein, 1977 and 1979; Krasner, 1985). It produced an offspring in the Conference on International Economic Cooperation (CIEC), which was conceived rather differently by the parties. The French initiators probably saw it mainly as an attempt to arrive at a political compromise between OPEC (export pricing) and OECD (supply guarantee) interests. Most LDCs – of which only a few were invited to take part – saw it as an attempt to defuse the agenda of the NIEO. The United States probably looked upon it as a typical French detour from the real political issues at stake[5].

The NIEO as well as the CIEC process eventually ended in a minimum solution as far as the whole package is concerned and a much weakened compromise on the ICP, which was eventually barely put to work.[6] We shall look more closely into the possible causes of this outcome below. It appears quite clear, however, that the 1980s have been dominated by other guiding principles than the one that the South held and for which they had for some time the support of many countries in the North – the socalled "like-minded" – and that the coming to the fore of these principles was one reason for the fall of the NIEO platform:

(4) *The re-emergence of the self-regulating market.* This is characteristic of the 1980s sub-period. It came as a result of the successful assault on Keynesian economic policies conducted by monetarism, supply side economics and neo-liberal ideas echoed by American and British administrations from the end of the 1970s on (Toye, 1987). It led to the demise of the NIEO agenda. It was closed not only because the leverage that the "Group of 77" (the South) had been able to exercise in the mid-1970s eroded, but because it was at odds with the new prevailing economic ideology. The shift of ideological hegemony that took place at the time of Bretton Woods and the Havana Charter thus appeared to have been repeated 30 years later.

Those ICAs that had been concluded and operated outside of the IPC were still operational, but they had serious problems (coffee, cocoa, tea, sugar, wheat, and tin). Some of them were in fact non-operational for long periods. Worst hit was the one ICA that apparently could claim to have had the longest-lasting success – the International Tin Agreement[7]. Its "success" turned out to a large extent to be based on the belief that negotiated price ranges could be defended almost indefinitely by debt-financed purchases of national commodity production to the ITA buffer stock. Moreover, the ITA's early achievements were preconditioned by large US purchases of tin for the national strategic stockpile. As the stockpile eventually contained tin metal corresponding to several times the annual global consumption, and contextual primarily geopolitical arguments to maintain purchases were gradually disappearing, demand slumped below the "normal" and surplus capacity became a serious obstacle to continued redistributive management.

To sum up this first stab at the empirical question, both contextual systemic factors, domestic political processes, and macroeconomic policy shifts influenced the negotiations over and the implementation of international commodity regimes. According to one comprehensive study, the UN processes and the ICAs facilitated regulatory accords and provided for greater transparency ... [and] also promoted compliance with the rules of agreements by monitoring states' behavior and offering forums in which the subject can be discussed. However ... neither these institutions nor other aspects of the regime have fundamentally altered international commodity trade or prompted states to change their policies to any significant degree. There is some evidence that states have continued to support ICAs for short periods of time because of a desire to avoid the political crises attendant on their collapse. But it is also clear that when important trading states realize that accords are definitely contrary to their interests, they are not reluctant to withdraw. (Finlayson and Zacher, p. 294)

More on the explanandum

Our discussion so far has treated the dependent variable rather intuitively and ad hoc – an approach that is also found in much of the literature on commodity regimes. Some degree of clarification is therefore required.

There is, for instance, a bias as to what *type* of institutionalized pattern of cooperation is to be expected. Thus there is a preference for hierarchical as opposed to non hierarchical institutions, and for a hierarchical preference structure as well. The goal was defined in terms of fixed measurable indicators of targets to be met by an agreement rather than defining the dependent variable more flexibly as the outcome of a continuous bargaining process. Failure to meet the targets was seen as an unsuccessful outcome of the cooperative effort.

This approach to commodity market regulation favoring centralized authority in combination with fixed numerical targets, which I take to be characteristic of the redistributive regulation approach to the NIEO and the IPC, should be subject to closer scrutiny. I shall return to reasons why it may still have some validity, but let the *auditur et altera pars* principle initiate the following observations.

The "inflexible centralization" approach to regulation may unduly and erroncously be confusing ends and means. For reasons, first, of a long-term secular decline in the net barter terms of trade of primary commodity exporters (Maizels, 1988) and, secondly, of "imperfect markets" (e.g. monopoly profits associated with oligopolistic coordination by firms and/or vertical integration in commodity production and distribution), some redistributive effort is needed in order to obtain equity. But it does not logically follow that centralization of the regulatory effort is indisputably and absolutely necessary. A case can be made for a less centralizing and a more flexible approach.

First, negotiations over international regimes are expected to be able to produce tangible results in terms of reducing information costs, increasing communication, and enhancing learning capacity (Keohane, 1984). There is very little doubt that the processes and institutions referred to above have produced reduced transaction costs in this sense. It is more open to discussion for how many participants they produced the same message and lesson (consensual knowledge) and for how long a period (stable consensus).

Secondly, the entry of new actors into markets that were previously relatively closed also meant that transactions became more transparent. Such increased market transparency was exploited by the OPEC countries from around 1970, by some bauxite-producing countries (such as Jamaica), and by others. But as they were associated with demands for redistributive regulation under some degree of centralized (multilateral) authority, quests for greater transparency by LDCs were at the same time mostly met with resistance or outright suspicion by the other side. Only a purely information-gathering and -disseminating enterprise such as the International Committee on Tungsten (under UNCTAD auspices) functioned without any apparent defection problem.

Thirdly, a case can be made theoretically for applying a decentralized approach to implementing redistributive regulation. One reason is that international agreements are based on voluntary commitment. Multilateral global arrangements usually require considerable resources for monitoring that participants do not defect. The operators of the tin agreement apparently in order to maintain the support of some key producers became involved in a spiral of debt-financed purchases to the buffer stock in order to defend a support price which moved away from that indicated by market trends. There is some reason to believe that a final price collapse could have been avoided by a more self-regulating market.

Another argument for decentralization is that centralizing global arrangements may adopt targets that reflect the principle of the "least common denominator." The effect of that would in cases where the redistributive goal has to be set high, be that resources for redistribution become inadequate. In other cases (and again tin may be a good example) the target is met at unrealistically high costs and the arrangement becomes economically non-sustainable. Other and basically decentralized arrangements such as framework agreements, binding selfcommitment or even bilateral (reciprocity-based), regional, or collective group arrangements (or combinations of them) may under given circumstances work better in these respects (Yarbrough and Yarbrough, 1987; Hveem, 1993).

The implication of this is that we should delink the issue of organization and institutional solution from that of the goal (end purpose, scope, etc.) of the cooperative endeavor. The empirical issue for the dependent variable is whether or not the goal is met; the institutional issue belongs under the explanans.

Reviewing the explanans

The configuration of actors' *interests* is the starting point in the analysis of commodity regulation politics. But exactly what sort of interests are prominent and shape the behavior of participants? The answer to that question is also an answer to the question: What role do issue characteristics play in explaining commodity politics?

An analysis of politics in the post World War II era naturally begins with the policies of the hegemonic state. To some of our respondents[8], the role of the United States in North–South politics during the Reagan–Bush administrations was that of a fairly consistent vetoing power to Southern demands, a role it did not play in the past. In his neorealist analysis of American commodity policies, Krasner (1978) identifies three clusters of interest: security of supply for the economy, minimization of prices paid by consumers, and broad foreign policy goals associated with national security. As Krasner himself correctly observes, these themes have been recurrent over time, but differing emphasis has been put on them. They do also tend to conflict. If one picks up from his analysis, which covered a period up to the mid-1970s, and from his conclusion that private business never dominated the policies of the state, which, on the contrary, was able to pursue a consistent preference structure of its own, some propositions for the analysis of the 1980s and 1990s can be deduced from his own inductive analysis.

First, the consistency and the relative strength of the three types of interest may both have changed, perhaps quite considerably. Krasner points to the decline of US hegemony (within a hegemonic stability theory perspective) as a source of uncertainty that he thought was likely to produce more domestic conflict over policy preferences. Although he may have exaggerated US decline and his assumption of hegemonic stability should be questioned, he was right in predicting change in the relative importance of the different elements in the interest configuration.

The coincidence of NIEO demands for redistributive regulation, international stagflation and surplus capacity problems, and successful monetarist attacks on Keynesian macroeconomic policies brought economic efficiency (price) considerations to the forefront at the end of the 1970s. In addition, increasing competition and a relative decline in American competitiveness in some sectors led the state to put more emphasis on economic rivalry with its allies and on protecting the competitiveness of American firms. As the East–West divide had ceased to be a major contextual factor in commodity policy-making at the end of the 1980s, the relative decline of security policy as opposed to broad national as well as specific *economic* interests as a priority concern of the state also appears to have been strengthened (Hveem, 1993).

In his other major study of commodity politics (1985), Krasner apparently fails to follow up the logic he developed in the first study. He correctly observes that the conflict of interest between the North and the South was as much or more political in nature than economic; it was a conflict over power and control of North–South exchanges. And he observed what appeared so obvious at the time the debt crisis erupted: increased vulnerability of (most parts of) the South made its quest for control even more logical. But he misread the consistency or tenacity of the Southern position and failed therefore to see the weakness of his own predicament about Southern strategy. He may not only have exaggerated the degree to which the South opposed liberal policies in the 1970s, but failed completely to predict the scope and consistency with which the South turned to accept liberal policy in the mid and late 1980s[9].

Rothstein implicitly includes interest-based analysis of the issue conflict formation in his explanation of NIEO failures, but combines it with an institutional and a process-oriented view. The efforts failed according to Rothstein mainly because the parties were unable to agree on procedural rules. That inability he ascribes to "structural, institutional, and intellectual obstacles" and the unwillingness of parties to make "concessions from beliefs and principles that are very firmly held" (Rothstein, 1979, p. 276). His suggested equilibrium point for the bargaining outcome would have been a compromise where the North offered some redistributive effort to meet legitimate Southern expectations, whereas the South would have to settle for incrementalism and gradualism in setting up "dependable rules" for the operation of the redistributive effort.

What can be deduced from all this? If we leave aside structural and cyclical explanations for a moment: Was the problem not only cognitive dissonance in the way parties defined the problem, or the divergence of interests that we have elaborated above, but also technical processual obstacles, timing (related to both economic and cognitive cycles), or the lack of consensual knowledge?

Participants in the actual bargaining process do tend to emphasize processual factors, such as proper timing of initiatives, the working out of consensual knowledge, the presence of competent solution-oriented entrepreneurs, and so on. As an example, high-ranking persons in the Norwegian Ministry of Foreign Affairs put strong emphasis on recruiting reputable economists to the ring of NIEO and IPC supporters, apparently in an effort to build the particular type of consensual knowledge thought decisive in laying the basis for a successful negotiating outcome. Mere political consensus-building to which the Norwegian government along with other "like-minded" countries contributed during the IPC negotiations, was not considered sufficient. Other officials in these countries have emphasized that not enough time was given for the process to build; the international and domestic context of politics demanded quick solutions on a win–lose basis, which prevented compromising from working[10].

The role of the entrepreneur has been emphasized in several recent studies (e.g. Young, 1989) and is illustrated even in the case of commodities. The agreement on setting up the International Natural Rubber Organization was the only successful result of the ICP attempt to construct individual commodity agreements. One important reason for the success may have been the role played in the negotiations by a few key people. One of them, Malaysia's Peter Lai, has been involved in several commodity negotiations, including the International Cocoa Organization during renegotiations in early 1993. The fact that Malaysia is not a member of the organization[11] has not prevented the United Nations from hiring his services. This proves that there is a small number of professional, highly respected negotiators who are being asked to take their experience across various individual commodity negotiations.

These explanations are no doubt of some value. Consensual

knowledge or the emergence of an "epistemic community" generally is to be considered an advantage. Our assumption is, however, that it is hard to find situations where it can be considered a sufficient, or even a primary condition for successful agreement. As an example, the terms-of-trade issue appears after a lengthy debate to have been more or less settled by the economic community: there is now fairly general consensus that there *is* a tendency toward a negative trend for the commodity exporters. Action in favor of redistributive regulation has not followed from that consensus. Income support programmes for producers and price support, including indexation of prices, were and still are rather widespread in most developed economies. But few of these economies were ready to transpose this practice from the domestic to the global market.

Even within the scope of environmentally related international agreements, broad consensual knowledge is not a sufficient condition for the successful conclusion and/or operation of an agreement, nor is it able to prevent a change of policy in a change-hostile environment. Even when strong political players enjoy almost general support from the scientific community, the process can produce an outcome to which this coalition is opposed[12].

Where then is the clue? We shall argue that it may be found in combining a small set of variables, the relative importance of each variable varying with structural conditions and whether or not these conditions change, with economic and political–ideological cycles, and with the way the variables interact.

An institutional argument

Two dimensions are particularly helpful in organizing the analysis: the dimension of *state vs. market* logic; and the dimension of *common vs. private property rights*.

The state–market distinction is represented with gross simplification by the dimension we introduced above – redistributive vs. competitive (self-administered) regulation. The second dimension may require a brief comment. A good is a private property when an individual actor who produces, distributes, buys, or sells that good can exclude others from having access to it. Alternatively a good is private property if others are not suffering from any externalities being forced on them as a result of the good being made use of by individual actors. Correspondingly, a good is considered common property if nobody can be excluded from access to it (alternatively, if everybody suffers under the externalities).

A large number of the primary commodities are site-bound goods, access to which can be made exclusive through the institution of private property. Some are also finite (non renewable, subject to available assessment of reserves) and some are renewable. But since it is a widely held view that they have a value only in the market, and a number of other private owners control access to the same commodity in their respective sites, the issue of privatization vs. commonization is transformed to take on a completely different meaning. The focal points for the configuration of actors' interests become price, ability to sell (market share), and guarantee to buy (supply availability).

We may represent the arena for the interaction of the variables on the two dimensions in terms of a simple fourcornered model (Figure 3.1).

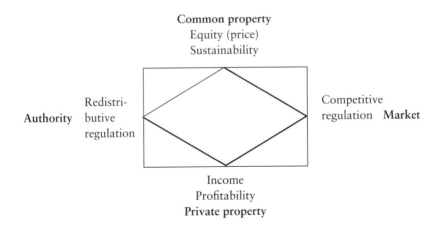

Figure 3.1

The problems of coordination and North–South collaboration in commodity markets may be highlighted in the following representation of the extreme bargaining positions on both sides.

The "radical" Southern position viewed both redistributive regulation through centralized multilateral price controls and not just national, but state control over property rights as a prerequisite for a viable agreement. It would thus combine demands for strong ICAs with demands for national state control over natural resources (socializing private property rights), in some cases even producer collaboration to support price demands through export controls, as in the case of OPEC.

The "radical" Northern position viewed competitive regulation through a decentralized market as a clearly superior and thus absolutely preferred arrangement and the institution of private property rights as not only economically superior (efficiency terms), but legally above politics and thus not subject to negotiation.

These ideal-type positions were reflected in reality, and they were probably quite influential poles of attraction on both sides. They therefore probably played an important role in preventing consensus-building within each of the two camps, as well as between them, from working out. We have to view the ICP negotiations within the larger context of the NIEO debate and the attempted "opecization" of commodities by the South. In linking the issue of property rights and the state vs. market issue directly or indirectly to commodity politics, moderating forces on both sides came under cross-fire and thus became weakened. As an example, the group of Northern "like-minded" countries could not go along with Southern thinking on the two dimensions, and they turned down almost all invitations to join producer associations initiated by the South (Hveem, 1978, 1979). Despite moderating forces on both sides and efforts by Southern negotiators in the IPC to dismiss the impression that they were out to "socialize the markets," the more skeptical on the Northern side were able to organize a winning coalition with the support of domestic interests associated with private property rights and their established market positions.

The South's negotiators were not without bargaining chips. First, they were able to set the agenda since the issue of commodity politics had been left to the UN and delegated to UNCTAD, not to GATT or Bretton Woods. This agenda-setting advantage – an aspect of meta-power – was contested by some of the major countries of the North and only reluctantly accepted by them. Secondly, the South appears to have managed better whenever it was able to coordinate individual country interests and stick to a common position. Success in this respect appears to have been greatest in commodities characterized not only by volatile prices, but by a tendency to demand downturns: coffee, tin, sugar, and cocoa. Less success was scored in those commodities that were characterized by a long-term tendency to falling prices (purchasing power): iron ore, phosphate rock, sisal, jute, tea, cotton, etc. (Finlayson and Zacker, 1988, pp. 262 ff).

The two types of price consideration, volatility and eroding purchasing power, should not be a reason for the South to collaborate more over the former commodities than over the latter. The fact that the former produced ICAs and the latter did not is probably as much due to differences in Northern attitudes. It is rather in line with an interest-based hypothesis that the North should be more inclined to favor agreement to avoid volatile prices than to avoid terms-of-trade trends that were moving in their own favor. Still the volatility argument was not sufficient to make the North agree to several more ICAs. One major reason is found by returning to the twodimensional model (Figure 3.1) and by turning to the two other aspects of the interest configuration referred to: market shares and supply predictability.

Many commodities were and still are characterized by private property rights closely linked to or institutionalized in transnational production and distribution organizations. Vertically integrated corporations and horizontal organization of distribution in long-term bilateral contracts, cartel-like arrangements, etc. dominate distribution channels in several minerals and many agricultural commodities. Changes have occurred, but not to the extent that this structure is basically altered in bauxite, iron ore, phosphate rock, bananas, and some other commodities. Such distribution channels normally do not offer easy transparency; information can still be maintained as private property. But some of them do offer a solution to price volatility. They have thus continued to attract Southern producers. In particular they have attracted weaker producers working under the threat of losing market share, whereas large producers, or smaller producers that stand to gain a larger market share, have been less inclined to link themselves. The latter also sometimes oppose ICAs that they see as restricting their chances of conquering larger market shares.

Bananas illustrate both the complexity of the issues and the dilemmas facing both the producing and the consuming end. In order to simplify the point a little, three different types of distribution channel confront the independent producers: fruit corporations, which are at the same time big producers themselves; the EU's Banana Protocol, which offers a number of countries guaranteed market shares in the Community; and the competitive market. The fruit corporations, which in combination with the corporations' intra-firm transfers are the channel that takes the biggest share of total banana trade, stand to gain from the liberalization agreed in the Final Agreement of the Uruguay Round in GATT because they will be in a better position than small non-integrated producers to serve an open competitive market. That leaves the EU's Banana Protocol, which is discriminatory according to GATT rules, but which offers a protected market to a number of small Caribbean economies where small-scale independent banana farming dominates. To make a further simplification: the choice appears to be between a multilateral arrangement that would almost certainly be captured by the fruit corporations and a "mini-lateral" one that, by discriminating in favour of producers other than those where corporate control prevails, helps producers to a guaranteed income.

Clientelism repeated? Or altruism on the part of the EU? Leaving that question aside, the issue has split the Community between the camp that prefers to follow the Uruguay Round philosophy and lift discriminatory measures, and on the other hand those who prefer to maintain the philosophy of the Protocol, thus favoring African, Caribbean, and Pacific members in the Caribbean and elsewhere, and impose quotas and above-quota tariffs on imports from Latin American countries[13].

The guaranteed market share that follows from a quota arrangement is a blend of private and common property, a *collective* property as it were. It is a value enjoyed by a group of actors, but not all; it is a result of discriminatory practice that offers redistributive regulation in favor of some. It is widely practiced, and it raises a still unresolved question: Can offering some part of the universe of needing a good be defended from a justice point of view?

Is there hope in "greening" production and distribution channels?

Our argument so far can be summarized to saying that private property is an intrinsic principle in commodity trade. Some of the factors that may help environmental agreements work, such as externalities, do not have a similar effect in the case of commodities. Competitive regulation can work in commodities, but the intensity of rivalry in consuming and in supplying markets is often very intense and makes market mechanisms fail. This happened to many commodities in the 1980s.

Redistributive regulation is very often dependent on political and moral arguments for its implementation and on a strong coalition of actors across conflicting interest formations to guarantee its enforcement. Often enforcement is more likely to succeed unilaterally or in bilateral or "mini-lateral" than in multilateral settings.

Could attempts to modify the factors that produce noncooperative outcomes be found in the recent tendency toward "greening" North–South relations and decision-making on production and distribution channels generally? We believe they marginally could. And in discussing that possibility we shall continue to use "North" and "South" as simplifying representations of Party and Counterpart, thus overlooking for the present purpose international divergences of views.

Attempts to make the distinction between renewable and non-renewable resources a matter for deciding on instituting common property vs private property rights were mostly unproductive in the past. The issue was never on the agenda of the NIEO and IPC negotiations. One important reason appears to have been the negative response to the Tragedy of the Commons and the Limits to Growth theses among Southern leaders in the 1970s. The response was in large measure motivated by a desire to maintain the option of exploiting raw materials as private property, whereas the message of the LTG was to view them as common property.

In an almost impermissible example of contrafactual analysis, one might observe that the South could have profited from going along with the LTG message if such a coalition had produced a basis for increasing and internalizing the discount rate for exhausting non-renewable resources. Such analysis excludes technological change and changing consumption patterns from being considered as a cause of commodity policy. That is clearly unacceptable: material saving technology, new materials including composites, cross-substitutability, and flexibility in sourcing supply have all affected commodity markets since the NIEO process started (Hveem, 1980. Some of the basis for the LTG message is thus eroded.

The 1980s produced a new appreciation of resource issues and also put many new resource types on the agenda, such as genetic material, the value of biodiversity, forests as climate-stabilizing resources, etc. This new appreciation has been mediated by the concern over, in particular, climate change. As we have seen above, this agenda transformation produced a potential for rearranging the private vs. common property dimension in favor of the latter, or possibly by the two converging. But exactly how and how much is still an open issue. We face two questions: first, what exactly speaks in favor of such a rearrangement; secondly, whether or not it makes cooperation between South and North more likely.

The suggested improved chance of cooperative solutions is premised, on the assumption, first, that the North finds arriving at an agreement that improves the chances of preventing, say global warming more salient than it found the IPC or similar arrangements, and, secondly, that the South can use the increased interest that the North takes in something that the South controls (tropical rain forests, for example) as a bargaining chip. The Brandt Commission (1979) attempted in vain to convince reluctant Northern leaders that it would be in their own interest to arrive at some redistributive regulation that preserved the South's income and thus purchasing power playing thus on the export interests of the North. Has the South in fact been given an improved bargaining position, and if so is it prepared and able to use it to arrive at a cooperative solution?

Increased saliency means that an issue outcome becomes more decisive in the short run. But the point about resource conservation is often that it takes the long run into account: action to prevent deterioriation of nature or exhaustion of rare genetic material or endangered species must be taken now. Add the precautionary principle and the borderline between short- and long-run considerations becomes blurred. Even the kind of technological optimism that has led decision-makers to overlook warnings that resources are running out (there will always be technological solutions in the future in time for a given problem of potential overexploitation to be solved) may become less compelling if the precautonary principle rules. Thus the dilemmas described in Figure 3.1 are reduced and partly solved (Figure 3.2).

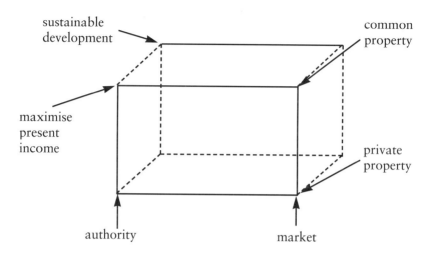

Figure 3.2 Sustainability as an incentive for cooperation[14]

The assumption of an improved bargaining position appears to be premised not only on increasing saliency, but on a potential convergence of preferences between the North and the South – and between protagonists of redistributive and of self-administered regulation.

Under the assumption that the South may play the game of issue linkage in a context of variable-sum games, the South could use the greatly enhanced interest that the North puts on climate policy to obtain concessions, e.g. on commodity policy. Or, if the issue is rather a matter of getting a satisfactory increase in the national income, the South could compensate for a lack of concessions on commodities by taking increased revenue out on the environment issues.

The UN Conference on Environment and Development (UNCED) process and the way the two resulting conventions are implemented will give us a clue to the answer. But some crucial questions remain. Resource and environment politics is, as much as is commodity politics, a two-level game: a process of continuous interaction between negotiations at the international level and bargaining at the domestic level. Strong distributive coalitions or particular interests may act as veto groups at the domestic level. Some private property rights are opposed to any change, while others may favor it. Issue-linkage may make this process very complex and eventually lead to stalemate. This type of explanation – public policy as a result of tough inter-administrative and inter-sectoral bargaining intensified by strongly activist NGOs – appears relevant to account for the fact that the United States has repeatedly cast a veto on occasions where a global consensus is sought.

This is where consensual knowledge may still be important. An important area of future research appears to be to identify clusters of interests that may form, or be brought together through information to form, coalitions in favor of long-term strategies. The GATT process, as has UNCED, produced new coalitions across the North–South divide that were not found, or probably to a limited degree even sought, during the NIEO process (Kahler and Odell, 1989). If this applies at the level of governments, it should be added that the potentially important role of NGOs is probably underestimated.

If interests are coalescing, if the experts agree with the policymakers and both are supported by representative NGOs, and all this uniting takes place at the international as well as at the domestic level, then the matching of opportunities for viable cooperation is perfect. But since such a maximally advantageous situation practically never occurs, the optimal strategy would be seeking a sufficient knowledge-based consensus, a winning coalition of policymakers, and the support of all but the more particularistic NGOs, and then attempting to achieve optimal timing of the context within which the proposal for common action is floated. In such optimal circumstances, structural impediments can be overcome, including vetoing hegemons, and the institutional solution can be non-hierarchical, even perhaps experimenting with several different solutions. But it would greatly enhance the probability of success if some major actors, in particular hegemons, were prevented from free-riding.

Notes

1 See Underdal (Chapter 4 in this volume) for a discussion and clarification of the use of the term in the context of international agreements. Underdal (1992) also discusses what makes an international agreement "effective."

2 The production of compromise was more of a reality in relations between the United States and (Western) Europe, resulting in the Organization for European Economic Cooperation (OEEC), than in intra-hemispheric relations.

3 See for instance, Perroux (1963) for an economic theory of the role of gifts in international relations.

4 Mention could be made of: the outcome of the Vietnam war; the reactions to the coup in Chile and allegations that ITT and the CIA were behind it; and the radicalization of some governments in the South with a record of being active in foreign affairs, such as Algeria, Jamaica, Libya, and Tanzania.

5 The French mostly, but not all the time, voted with the United States, the United Kingdom, and Japan against the NIEO principles, but appear to have had second thoughts from time to time owing to their particular responsibilities toward their African clients.

6 The Common Fund was formally voted in 1982, but it took six years to get a sufficient number of countries ratify it. A site for the headquarters was found (Netherlands), and the fund appears finally to be operational as of the early 1990s. The lack of progress in setting up individual ICAs however – the ICP process in fact produced only one, in natural rubber – means that the programme is hardly functioning yet.

7 See Hveem (1976), where the efficiency of the ITA was questioned. The skeptical remarks were commented upon in a quite unusual editorial by the editor of *Revue Tiers Monde* (where it was published), who made a sort of disclaimer. Although it may have been for several more reasons than the one observed by me that the ITA went virtually bankrupt in the 1980s, the fall provides *ex post facto* support for my conclusion.

8 I refer to interviews conducted with a select number of high-ranking negotiators mostly from Nordic and a couple of other "like-minded" countries or "middle-powers" (Pratt, 1989).

9 See Rothstein (1988) for a similar critique.

10 These observations are based on interviews with a select number of Nordic (mostly Norwegian) officials who took part in the IPC process and have experience both of Law of the Sea negotiations and of GATT.

11 Indonesia and Malaysia among the big producers and the United States among the consuming countries are not members.

12 An illustration is the convention on radioactive waste dumping, which effectively prevented ocean dumping from being continued despite the fact that most of the research world was telling politicians that ocean radwaste dump-

ing represented no serious threat to humans, and despite the fact that several influential governments, including the US administration, opposed a ban on dumping. The effective cessation of dumping in the middle of the 1980s was a result of popular pressure organized by environmentalists in the United States and spanning an international coalition including politicians in several countries (Ringius, 1992).

13 The matter appears to have been taken to a GATT panel by the Latin American countries concerned (see *Financial Times*, 11 February 1993).

14 This three-dimensional perspective was suggested to me by Robert O. Keohane.

References

Brandt Commision (1979) *North-South: A Programme for Survival.* (The Report of the Independent Commision on International Development Issues)

Emmanuel, Arghiri (1978) *Unequal Exchange* (New York: Monthly Review Press).

Finlayson, Jock A., and Mark W. Zacher (1988) *Managing International Markets. Developing Countries and the Commodity Trade Regime* (New York: Columbia University Press).

Haas, Peter (1989) "Do Regimes matter? Epistemic Communities and Mediterranean pollution control," *International Organization*, vol. 43, no. 3 (Summer), pp. 349–76.

Hveem, Helge (1975) "Les mateères premières, les accords maultilateraux et la structure du pouvoir economique," *Revue Tiers Monde*, 66, avril-juin.

Hveem, Helge (1977) *En ny økonomisk verdensorden og Norge* [A New International Economic Order and Norway] (Oslo: Universitetsforlaget).

Hveem, Helge (1978) *The Political Economy of Third World Producer Associations* (Oslo: Scandinavian Universities Press).

Hveem, Helge (1979) "Scandinavia, the Likeminded Countries, and the New International Economic Order," in E. Laszlo and Joel Kurtzman, eds. *Western Europe and the New International Economic Order* (New York: Pergamon Press), pp. 54–96.

Hveem, Helge (1980) "The World Copper Industry." Consultancy report for the UNCTAD Secretariat, mimeo.

Hveem, Helge (1993) "Hegemonic Rivalry and Antagonistic Interdependence. Managed Trade and Bilateralism in International Trade." Centre for Development and the Environment.

Kahler, Miles, and John Odell (1989) "Developing Country Coalition-Building and International Trade Negotiations," in John Whalley, ed., *Developing Countries and the Global Trading System* (London: Macmillan), vol. I, pp. 149–70.

Keohane, Robert O. (1984) *After Hegemony. Cooperation and Discord in the World Political Economy* (Princeton; NJ: Princeton University Press).

Krasner, S. D. (1978) *Defending the National Interest. Raw Materials Interests and US Foreign Policy* (Princeton; NJ: Princeton University Press).

Krasner, S.D. (1985) *Structural Conflict. The Third World Against Global Liberalism* (Berkeley: University of California Press).

Mark, Janette, and Ann Weston (1989) "The Havana Charter Experience: Lessons for Developing Countries," in John Whalley, ed., *Developing Countries and the Global Trading System* (London: Macmillan), vol. I, pp. 45–65.

Paley Commission on Supplies and Shortages (1952) *Government and the Nation's Resources* (Washington DC: Government Printing Office).

Prebisch, Raul (1949) *The Economic Development of Latin America and Some of Its Problems* (New York: ECLA).

Ravenhill, John (1985) *Collective Clientelism. The Lomé Conventions and North–South Relations* (New York: Columbia University Press).

Ringius, Lasse (1992) *Radwaste Disposal and the Global Ocean Dumping Convention: The Politics of International Environmental Regimes*, PhD thesis (Florence: The European University Institute).

Rothstein, Robert L. (1979) *Global Bargaining. UNCTAD and the Quest for a New International Economic Order* (Princeton, NJ: Princeton University Press).

Rothstein, Robert L. (1988) "Epitaph for a Monument to a Failed Protest? A North–South retrospective," *International Organization*, vol. 42, no. 4 (Autumn), pp. 725–48.

Singer, Hans W. (1950) "The Distribution of Gains between Investing and Borrowing Countries," *American Economic Review: Papers and Proceedings* (May).

Underdal, Arild (1992) "The Concept of Regime Effectiveness'", *Cooperation and Conflict*, vol. 27, no. 3, pp. 227–40.

Yarbrough, Beth, and Robert Yarbrough (1986) "Reciprocity, Bilateralism, and Economic Hostages: Self-enforcing Agreements in International Trade," *International Studies Quarterly*, vol. 30, pp. 7–21.

Young, Oran R. (1989) "The Politics of International Regime Formation: Managing Natural Resources and the Environment," *International Organization*, vol. 43, pp. 349–75.

Measuring and Explaining Regime Effectiveness

Arild Underdal

Many of the major policy challenges facing governments today are in some sense *collective* problems, calling for *joint* solutions. Even when effective solutions can be developed and implemented *only* through joint efforts, voluntary cooperation can, however, be hard to establish and sustain. The fact that effective collective action can be so hard to bring about makes it all the more important to understand the conditions for "success" and the causes of "failure." Why are some international problems solved more effectively or easily than others? Or, put differently: Why do some efforts at developing and implementing joint solutions "succeed" while others "fail"?

This paper is an effort to undertake some of the conceptual groundwork required for analyzing this general question. I shall proceed in two steps. The first is to explore the meaning of "success" in this context; what precisely do we mean when we say that a problem-solving effort "succeeds" or that a solution is "effective"? The second part of the paper will suggest a very crude model for *explaining* "success" and "failure."

The dependent variable: the concept of regime "effectiveness"

In the study of international cooperation, a problem-solving effort has often been considered a success if it leads to some kind of collaborative arrangement (in particular if that arrangement constitutes a new or stronger "regime"). At least two good reasons can be given for trying to develop a more sophisticated concept of regime *effectiveness*.

One is simply that equating success with the establishment of *any* kind of cooperative arrangement would lead us to focus on formal rather than substantive achievements. Even an international regime including an elaborate set of formal injunctions may be a very weak institution indeed, accomplishing little or nothing in terms of substantive problem-solving. Conversely, a negotiation process that does not lead to full agreement may have achieved significant progress on a politically very "malign" problem (Underdal, 1992). If our real concern is problem-solving, it may be perfectly sensible to rate the latter as "more successful" than the former.

Another reason for shifting research priorities is that we do not yet have adequate conceptual tools for measuring regime "effectiveness." The present state of the art is characterized by a fair amount of conceptual disarray. One of the options that have been frequently used in previous research is to focus on formal properties, notably *level of cooperation*, usually defined in terms of the kind of functions fulfilled (information exchange, rule-making, rule enforcement, etc., see e.g. Kay and Jacobson, 1983, pp. 14–18). Level of cooperation may be positively correlated with, and in fact causally related to, problem-solving "effectiveness," but the link is hardly compelling. The fact that a regime includes substantive regulations does not tell us anything about the "clout" of those regulations. Another strategy that has been used in previous research is to focus on procedural indicators, such as the extent to which the work of an international organization proceeds as scheduled (see Jacobson and Kay, 1983, pp. 316–17), or the speed and rate of ratifications. Again, these are crude and unreliable indicators of substantive "effectiveness"; in fact, one might even suspect that the speed of ratification may be *inversely* related to regulatory clout. More promising are some notions of regime "strength," including the one(s) suggested by Aggarwal

(1985, p. 20), and Zacker (1987, p. 177).[1] But recent literature provides us with *different* concepts of regime "strength"[2], so great care is required before making inferences from term to concept. Before plunging into large-scale comparative studies, a fair amount of conceptual groundwork therefore seems required to clarify what precisely is our dependent variable. This section of the paper offers some quite tentative reflections on that question.

Most basically, evaluating the "effectiveness" of a cooperative arrangement means *comparing* something – let us provisionally refer to this object simply as "the regime" – against some standard of success or accomplishment. Any attempt at designing a framework for the study of regime effectiveness must, then, cope with at least three (sets of) questions: (1) What precisely constitutes *the object* to be evaluated? (2) Against which *standard* is this object to be evaluated? (3) *How* do we operationally go about comparing the object with our standard; in other words, what kind of measurement operations do we have to perform in order to attribute a certain *score* of "effectiveness" to a certain object (regime)? Let us briefly consider these three questions.

What constitutes the object to be evaluated?

The answer may at first thought appear obvious; the object clearly must be the arrangement in focus. On second thoughts, however, it becomes abundantly clear that this answer does not take us very far. Let us therefore briefly consider the main options before us.

First, we shall have to determine whether we are interested only in the (impact of) the substantive arrangement itself or also in the costs incurred and positive side-effects generated in the efforts to establish and maintain it. The former is the appropriate basis for evaluating the *regime* itself, while the latter provides a basis for evaluating *problem-solving efforts*. The distinction is not merely one of academic "hair-splitting." Establishing and operating a regime usually entail costs, and rational actors presumably make their choices on the basis of some estimate of net benefits. Now, it seems that most governments, at least in the industrialized world, in fact tend not to be much concerned about transaction costs in the most basic sense (salaries, office costs, travel and accommodation expenses, etc.); less tangible "political" costs seem to get more attention. But problem-solving efforts can also have significant "positive" side-effects. Consider briefly the process of developing coordinated policies for controlling anthropogenic sources of global climate change. The domestic and international preparations have been a large-scale exercise in *learning*. Decision-makers have acquired a better understanding of the problem, and are now in a better position to make "enlightened" decisions than they were a few years ago. In the process they may have discovered no-regret options that can be pursued by unilateral action. The fact that the problem has become a matter of serious international negotiations itself affects expectations as well as incentives. Emitters of greenhouse gases may expect policy changes (for instance the introduction of a CO_2 tax) and try to adjust accordingly, and companies involved in the development of environmentally "benign" sources of energy may make additional investments in preparation for what they see as new opportunities. Furthermore, the mere existence of an arena such as the UN Conference on Environment and Development (UNCED) Summit provides incentives to political leaders to come up with policy initiatives responding to the official purpose and the "atmosphere" of the conference. The aggregate impact of such side-effects may very well be as important as the impact of the formal conventions and declarations signed at the end (see Underdal, 1993). To make our task manageable, we shall in this paper focus mainly on the (consequences of) the regime itself. But the overall implication of what we have said above should not be missed: problem-solving efforts usually generate their own consequences, separate from those that can be attributed to the regime they may establish. And some of these process-generated costs and side-effects may, indeed, be far from trivial.

Second, we should also ask ourselves whether we want to conceive of "success" only in terms of the (net) benefits produced, or in terms of the more elusive notion of "achievement," the difference being that in the latter case success is "weighted" by taking into account also the "malignity" of the problem in focus. In this paper I shall adopt the former perspective, but we should recognize that for some purposes – e.g. evaluating the prospects for "solving" a certain problem – the latter perspective would provide the more interesting construct. Other things being equal, the more "malign" the problem, the more it takes to solve it, and the greater would be the achievement of solving it. Thus, the problem of controlling anthropogenic sources of global climate change is certainly far more complex and arguably also significantly more "malign" (in political terms) than, for example, the problem of preventing the depletion of stratospheric ozone. From this statement it follows that more intellectual and institutional capacity and a greater amount of "political energy" will be required to achieve the "same" level of "effectiveness."

Third, as Easton (1965, pp. 351–2) and others remind us, a distinction should be made between the *output* of a decision-making process (i.e. the norms, principles, and rules constituting the regime itself) and the set of consequences flowing from the implementation of and adjustment to that regime (here referred to as *impact*).[3] The former focuses on the phase of regime creation, while the latter takes us into the stage of regime implementation and maintenance. In the end, impact will normally be the more important concern. The actual impact of a regime or a regulation can, however, be determined only in retrospect – meaning several years after its entry into force.[4] If we want to evaluate regime effectiveness at an earlier stage – as we often do – the regime itself will be all that is known to us. In such a situation we should realize that predicting impact on the basis of data only about output will not necessarily be a straightforward exercise. In cases where regulations are of the "command-and-control" type, we at least know (more or less precisely) which kinds of behavior are prescribed, permitted, or prohibited. But actors do sometimes respond by more or less flagrant non-compliance or by making ingenious adjustments that may be hard to predict. In cases where some instrument for manipulating incentives (e.g. pollution charges) is being used, all we know is the additional costs that actors are supposed to pay for a certain amount of "unwanted" behavior (or the additional benefits promised as a reward for behaving "well"). How, and how strongly, actors will in fact respond to a certain change in the structure of incentives may be an open question. Two general implications for the study of regime effectiveness seem to be, first of all, that we need to specify explicitly whether we are referring to output or to impact,[5] and, secondly, that great caution is required in attempting to infer impact from data only about output.

Against which standard is the arrangement to be evaluated?

Defining an evaluation standard involves at least two main steps: one is to determine the point of reference against which actual achievement is to be compared, the other is to determine what might be called the "unit of measurement."

It seems that there are basically two points of reference that merit serious consideration in this context. One is the hypothetical state of affairs that would have come about had the regime not existed. This point of reference leads us to conceive of "effectiveness" in terms of relative improvement caused by the regime.[6] This is clearly the notion we have in mind when considering whether and to what extent "regimes matter." The other option is to evaluate a regime against some concept of *collective optimum*. This is the appropriate perspective if we want to determine to what extent a collective problem is in fact "solved" under present arrangements. Using potential achievement as our point of reference, we would define a "perfect" solution as one that accomplishes all that can be accomplished – given the state of knowledge at the time[7].

These two approaches are clearly complementary. Even a regime leading to a substantial improvement may fall short of being "perfect." Conversely, in more fortunate situations a minor adjustment may be quite sufficient to reach the collective optimum. Moreover, both dimensions are interesting in their own right; international regimes are, it seems, typically evaluated in terms of how well they (can be expected to) perform compared with the state of affairs that would have come about in their absence *as well as* in terms of their ability to solve the problems they are designed to cope with. This suggests that the student of international regimes needs to be able to play with *both* these notions of effectiveness, but also that it is critical not to confuse the two. This has important implications also with regard to terminology: referring to Figure 4.1, cases in the upper-right-hand corner may unambiguously be labelled "effective" and those in the lower-left-hand cell "ineffective." For mixed scores we need a richer set of labels.

	Distance to collective optimum	
	Great	Small
High	Important, but still imperfect	Important and perfect
Relative improvement		
Low	Insignificant and suboptimal	Unimportant, yet optimal

Figure 4.1 Two dimensions of "effectiveness"

Each of these approaches calls for further conceptual refinement. Consider, first, the notion of "relative improvement." Although intuitively meaningful, the provisional definition given above leaves open at least one critical question: What precisely is the baseline from which improvement should be measured?

In principle, it seems that we have a choice between two basic options. One is some hypothetical "state of nature" that would have obtained if, instead of the present regime, we were left in a "no-regime" condition.[8] The alternative option would be to take as our baseline the situation that would have existed had the previous "rules of the game" been left unchanged. The former measures effectiveness in "absolute" terms, while the latter focuses on incremental change (effectiveness "differentials"). For at least some analytical purposes, the former arguably provides us with the more interesting conceptualization, but at the same time it leaves us with the elusive notion of a "no-regime condition," with no clues as to how we should go about determining what such a condition would look like. If we choose the latter option, we would presumably be able to identify the state of affairs that we are talking about. However, our conception of effectiveness would be a strictly differential one, and the score that we attribute to any specific regime would be heavily influenced by the level of effectiveness obtained under the previous arrangement. And it certainly may be confusing to label a regime leading to a state of affairs close to the collective optimum "ineffective" simply because its "predecessor" was nearly as "good." This again suggests that we need a richer set of labels to distinguish *marginal change* in effectiveness from *absolute scores*.

The problems briefly outlined above indicate to me (a) that, although relative improvement may legitimately be considered an interesting and important aspect of effectiveness, it should be tempered or supplemented with some measure of how well actual achievement compares with the "optimal" solution; (b) that the "no-regime" condition may be considered the more fundamental baseline from which (relative) improvement should, if at all feasible, be measured; and (c) that scores obtained by using one baseline cannot – or only in special circumstances and then with great caution – be used interchangeably with scores derived from another baseline.

Conceiving of "effectiveness" in terms of the distance between what is actually accomplished and what could have been accomplished, given the state of knowledge at the time, immediately puts before us the intriguing question of what constitutes the maximum that can be accomplished. Whenever we are talking about joint solutions, the answer depends on the decision rule. If we assume that actors are free to choose *any* decision rule that they consider instrumental, the outer limit will be the solution(s) maximizing the *sum* of net benefits to the group. There are, however, several problems with this notion of joint maximum. One is that, if we conceive of benefits in terms of subjective utilities rather than objective "realia," this notion calls for inter-actor comparison of utilities – a methodological challenge that remains to be conclusively solved. More important here is the fact that it may rightly be dismissed as invalid for the decision rule typically used in inter-governmental dealings. Strictly interpreted, it applies only to the making of unilateral decisions by a perfectly unitary actor. Whenever we are dealing with collective decisions that can be made only through agreement, the appropriate notion of collective optimum is the Pareto frontier. This frontier is reached when no further increase in benefits to one party can be obtained without thereby leaving one or more prospective partner(s) worse off. In favorable circumstances, a solution maximizing the sum of net benefits will also be Pareto optimal, but there is no guarantee that the two frontiers will necessarily coincide. Accordingly, the choice between these two notions is not merely a quibble about labels.

It is not obvious which of these, or possibly other, notions of collective optimum is the more appropriate here. In favor of adopting the Pareto frontier it may be argued that the concern with regime effectiveness provides no role for some purely hypothetical frontier that is not generally achievable given the institutional constraints under which actors actually operate. To qualify as potential, a solution must be accessible within the kinds of settings that do in fact exist or can feasibly be brought about.

Although compelling in itself, this argument does not quite settle the case. It remains to be determined which decision rules can be considered available instruments in international politics. The general answer seems to be that governments are, in principle, free to adopt *any* decision rule that they *collectively* consider appropriate. The crux of this formulation is the word "collectively"; the choice of decision rule is itself a joint decision, and as such subject to the rule(s) for making such meta-decisions. This is equivalent to saying that any substantive decision rule will itself ultimately have to pass the threshold required by the rule governing its meta-decision. The answer may now be reformulated as follows: Governments are free to choose any decision rule that they can agree on, or can agree to determine by some other procedure. Agreement is not the only decision rule available to actors in international politics, but in a basically anarchical system it constitutes the requirement that any other decision rule will have to meet to be adopted. We may therefore conclude that – although transcendable for *specific* problem-solving efforts – the Pareto frontier may be considered the *ultimate* limit within which governments will have to build voluntary, cooperative arrangements.

In trying to apply the Pareto criterion to specific cases, we will soon discover that we are dealing with a sensitive instrument. The Pareto frontier can be determined only for a given negotiation setting, including a given set of actors and a certain set of issues and issue linkages (see for example Sebenius, 1983). A change in any of these elements may affect the range of politically feasible solutions. This renders the Pareto frontier less attractive for purposes of empirical research than it appears in abstract reasoning. In trying to apply this notion of collective optimum in empirical research, a student will therefore often have to resort to simplistic assumptions similar to those conventionally made in formal bargaining theory.

To define a standard of evaluation, not only do we need to decide upon a point of reference against which actual achievement is to be compared; we also need to define some standardized *metric of evaluation* or unit of measurement. In some cases the appropriate option may be quite obvious. In others, however, we seem to face a choice between measuring "effectiveness" in terms of human welfare (usually translated into economic efficiency) or in terms of ecological or technical properties.[9] For example, the (performance of the) International Whaling Commission (IWC) regime may be evaluated in terms of aggregate net economic benefits or in terms of aggregate biological yield over time or some preservationist notion of the rights or sanctity of Nature. The score that we would give to the IWC depends critically on which of these values we choose to base our evaluation metric. The most basic lessons seem to be that we should (a) be explicit about the choice we make, and (b) realize that scores obtained by using different evaluation metrics cannot be used interchangeably – at least not without a critical examination of compatibility.

How do we, in operational terms, attribute a certain score to a regime?

As each of the different approaches outlined above raises its own particular problems of measurement, this question is too complex to be pursued in depth here. Suffice it in this section to offer just a few introductory remarks intended mainly to identify the major methodological challenges to be faced.

Before submerging ourselves into the practicalities of empirical measurement, it seems appropriate to set our ambitions straight. At this stage, no attempt to go beyond *ordinal-level* measurement will be attempted. The basic purpose of our research – accounting for the "success" and "failure" of international problem-solving efforts – does not require higher-level measurement. Nor do I know how to construct a cardinal scale that would make sense in this context. In fact, the ordinal scale that we intend to use in the comparative analysis is truncated to include only three scores: "successes," "failures," and an intermediate category for cases that fall somewhere in-between. Even such a crude ordering of cases is by no means a straightforward exercise.

The major challenge that we face in moving from the conceptual to the empirical level of analysis is to attribute scores to phenomena that cannot be observed directly, but have to be inferred from information about some presumably related variable. More specifically, we face this kind of problem whenever we try to predict impact from information only about output, and in trying to determine empirically our point of reference – be it the collective optimum or the hypothetical state of affairs that would have existed in the absence of the regime in question. Suffice it here to say a few words about the point-of-reference problem.

If we conceive of effectiveness in terms of relative improvement, we need to determine what would have happened had the regime not existed. This is a counterfactual question. What we can empirically observe is the state of affairs that existed (immediately) before the regime was established (at time t_0). What we want to know, however, is the set of consequences that would have flowed from a continuation of the previous "rules of the game" (at times $t_{+1} \ldots t_{+n}$) or what would have happened under a "no-regime" condition. Information about the state of affairs existing at time t_0 may provide a *basis* for inferring at least the former, but it is important to keep in mind that it provides only a basis; it is not itself the piece of information that we want. One practical suggestion could be to look for whatever predictions we can find in negotiation documents, preferably documents that can be seen as "non-partisan" inputs. In the absence of such data, the task of determining what would otherwise have happened simply calls for the best judgment that the analyst can make herself, on the basis of available sources.

Determining the *maximum* that can be accomplished may be even more difficult. One sensible "rule of thumb" seems to be to look for independent expert advice indicating to decision-makers what would be the (technically) "perfect" solution. There are, though, several problems pertaining to this suggestion. One obvious constraint is that conclusive expert advice will not be available in all the cases that we want to study. Secondly, even where it is available it may be hard to translate into a yardstick for measuring effectiveness. This is so for at least two reasons: (1) it will probably refer to technical or ecological criteria, not to social welfare (which, presumably, is the principal concern of governments), nor will it conceive of the collective optimum in terms of political feasibility; (2) wherever no unequivocal threshold or target exists, advice may be framed in terms of different levels of ambition (for example, preventing further deterioration, restoring a stock or ecosystem in x years, etc.). Despite these and other pitfalls, expert advice submitted to decision-makers is clearly one source of data to be utilized. When expert advice cannot be found, or appears so inconclusive that no optimum can reliably be inferred, a fallback strategy may be to look for some official declaration of a joint goal or purpose. Some, but not all, conferences provide such a declaration (for example, "eradicate hunger in 10 years"). Whenever such a target is explicitly formulated, it may serve as a point of reference. It should be recognized, though, that the relationship between such a target and the "objective" optimum is by no means clear. This indicates that the latter strategy should be used with great caution, and that scores based on different strategies cannot be used interchangeably.

Recognizing that even with an elaborate manual the analyst will have to rely heavily on subjective and perhaps even somewhat impressionistic judgment, a strong case can be made for subjecting our own scores to some "external" test of reliability. Such a test may be organized as follows. Ask a sample of about 10 experts (e.g. civil servants, scholars) who know the issue well to score the regime in terms of relative improvement and distance from the "collective optimum" (these notions must, of course, be explained in some detail). The instrument may be e.g. a 5 or 10 point scale.

Compute the average score, and compare the score itself, as well as the ranking derived from scores for a set of cases, with your own. Whenever the referees disagree substantially among themselves, or the ranking derived from their scores differs significantly from your own, further examination of the case record seems required. Admittedly, such a procedure would be vulnerable since the referees would not themselves compare cases (or, at most, compare only a few cases). Using their scores as the basis for ranking cases therefore implies a strong assumption about inter-referee standardization of evaluation scales. This problem is, though, quite similar to one that any research team will have to face in its internal proceedings.

Concluding remarks

As indicated by the preliminary casestudies reported by Wettestad and Andresen (1991) as well as those reported by Miles (1991), the scores we end up with will sometimes depend on the exact definition of "effectiveness" that is applied. This observation raises two important questions.

First, does it make sense to try to develop some *composite* or *aggregate* score? This is itself a complex question. My own view can be summarized as follows:

(1) If we are talking about using different operational indicators for the same theoretical concept, computing some aggregate score basically means constructing an index. This may certainly be a sensible thing to do, provided that the indicators included are believed to capture different aspects of the phenomenon we are trying to get at.

(2) Aggregating scores across different basic concepts is a straightforward operation only as long as one case dominates another. For example, referring to Figure 4.1 (p. 98), I can see no problem

in rating cases in the upper-right-hand category as "more effective" than those in the lower-left-hand cell; in terms of my two criteria the former strongly dominates the latter. I would also be prepared to rate the two remaining cells as falling somewhere in-between these two extremes; they can both be seen as weakly dominated by cases in the upper-left cell, and do themselves weakly dominate cases in the lower-right-hand category. In order to produce some sensible aggregate score where one case does not dominate another, we would have to be able to translate units of "relative improvement" into units of "distance from the collective optimum." I can see no firm basis for performing such an exercise.

Second, can the same model or set of independent variables be used to account for variations in effectiveness – *irrespective of which definition we adopt*? Can, for example, the same model that is used to explain variations in what Young (1991) refers to as "effectiveness as problem solving" equally well account for variations in what he calls "process effectiveness" or "constitutive effectiveness"?[10] The wider the range of definitions, the less warranted seems to be such a sweeping assumption. The question seems, though, pertinent even with regard to the more limited range of options suggested in this paper. And it is not at all obvious that the answer is generally positive.

Moreover, any attempt at measuring effectiveness will refer to the state of affairs *at one particular point in time* (or for a limited period of time). Since producing effects usually takes time, the score that we attribute to a certain regime may depend upon the point in time at which it is observed. Everything else being the same, we would expect the effectiveness of a regime to increase when it has had the time to "mature" and penetrate the system of activities in question. (There is, though, no reason to expect a *monotonous* increase in effectiveness with regime age). One important implication of these observations is that comparing the impact of two or more regimes is a straightforward exercise only if these regimes are "measured" at similar stages in their "life cycles." Whenever we are not able to "synchronize" observations in this particular sense, great caution is required in comparing scores across cases.

The independent variables: what determines regime effectiveness?

At the most general level, there seem to be two main answers to the question why some international problems are solved more effectively or easily than others. One seeks the explanation in the character of the *problem* itself. The basic proposition is that some problems are more simple or "benign" than others, and hence easier to solve. The alternative hypothesis focuses on *problem-solving capacity*, the general argument being that some efforts are more successful than others because more powerful tools are being used or because the problem is attacked with greater skill and/or energy. The two are linked in the sense that what is required to solve a problem (i.e. what constitutes problem-solving capacity) may depend on the character of that problem. This makes the specification of problem-solving capacity all the more complex. In the basic model serving as my point of departure in this paper, however, I suggest that we conceive of regime effectiveness simply as a function of problem "benignity" and problem-solving capacity.

The two general propositions formulated above become interesting only if we can translate them into specific form. Suggesting that some problems are harder to solve than others is helpful only if we can specify *which* kinds of problems are hard to solve and what makes them so. Likewise, the proposition that "success" depends on problem-solving capacity becomes interesting only if we can specify *which* institutions or "tools" are the most effective devices, and why. Any attempt at pursuing these questions in depth would take me far beyond the scope of this paper. All I can offer here are some very tentative suggestions, aimed at pointing out some important determinants of problem malignancy and problem-solving capacity. I shall focus primarily on the elusive concept of "problem-solving capacity," the simple reason being that – thanks largely to developments in the field of game theory analysis – our understanding of what makes a problem politically "malign" seems at this stage to be far more advanced than our understanding of what determines our capacity to solve it.[11]

What makes a problem difficult to solve?

An international problem may be difficult to solve in at least two respects. First, a substantial amount of *intellectual* "capital" and energy may be needed to arrive at an accurate diagnosis and to develop a functionally adequate "cure." It is, for example, by no means obvious what level and pattern of resource exploitation can be expected to maximize the long-term social welfare that can be harvested from Antarctica. Nor is it clear what are the socially optimal levels of emission of various greenhouse gases. At another level, international problems are also *political* issues, and as such they can be more or less "malign." The political malignancy of a problem can be conceived of as a function of the configuration of actor preferences and beliefs. More precisely, at least two aspects of the configuration of preferences seem to be important: One is incongruity between the cost–benefit calculations of individual actors and that of the group of actors; the other is asymmetry between actor interests, and between costs and benefits.

To see how *incongruity* can affect actor incentives, let q_a be the fraction of the universe of benefits produced by a certain action that enters actor A's own cost–benefit calculations, and k_a be the corresponding fraction of the cost universe. If $q_a > k_a$, meaning that the actual costs are "underrepresented" in A's own calculations (as is the case in transfrontier pollution), A will himself tend to pursue that line of action "too far." Conversely, if $q_a < k_a$, meaning that only some of the actual benefits are included in A's calculus (as is the case with unilateral measures to mitigate global environmental problems), an option will appear as less attractive to the actor than it is to the group as a whole. Other things being equal, the larger the discrepancy between q_a and k_a, the more A's individual behavior will tend to deviate from what is required to achieve the collective optimum. This is the logic behind Mancur Olson's (1968, p. 29) well-known proposition that a "large" actor can be expected to behave more in line with "the common interest" than a "smaller" one. In what Olson calls a "privileged group," the individual cost–benefit calculations of the "largest" actor will be sufficiently close to that of the group to induce behavior that leads to the group optimum (Olson, 1968, pp. 49–50). By implication, incongruity need not lead to inefficiency but, if it becomes sufficiently large and "universal", all non-altruistic actors will behave in a way that makes aggregate benefits to the group fall short of its potential. When this happens, some form of corrective device will be needed to solve or alleviate the problem.

As indicated above, a problem can be *asymmetrical* in at least two respects. First, it can be asymmetrical in the sense that the parties involved are "coupled" so that their interests are negatively correlated. The typical upstream–downstream relationship is a case in point; unless some kind of cost-sharing scheme is established, measures to control unidirectional transfrontier pollution will benefit the "victims" at the expense of the polluters. Other things being equal, the greater the asymmetry in terms of the impact that different options will have on the actors involved, the more difficult it will be to work out a solution that is mutually acceptable. A problem may also be asymmetrical in that the character of the costs involved differs systematically from the character of the benefits. Thus, for a number of environmental problems the costs of pollution abatement tend to be easy to specify, close in time, and concentrated to specific groups or sectors of the economy, while benefits tend to be uncertain (in some cases even hypothetical), belong to a more or less distant future, and accrue to society at large (or be indeterminate in their social distribution).

Other things being equal, we would – in a business-as-usual scenario – expect the former set of consequences to generate more "political energy" than the latter.

Intellectual complexity and political malignancy may interact to make a problem intractable. Thus, uncertainty about the causes of the problem or about the impact of alternative solutions may fuel political controversy, and political controversy may in turn have negative repercussions for research and the development of consensual knowledge.

What determines problem-solving capacity?

Capacity is always the capacity to do *something*. Accordingly, problem-solving capacity can be determined precisely only with reference to some particular category of tasks and problems. All I can offer here will therefore be a very brief and general introduction intended only to identify the principal constitutive elements of the capacity to cope with the *political* intricacies of collective problems.

When solutions are to materialize as collective decisions, *problem-solving capacity* (more precisely, its political dimension) can be seen as a function of three major determinants: (1) the institutional setting, including the "rules of the game"; (2) the distribution of power among the actors involved; and (3) the skill and energy invested in the designing and marketing of cooperative solutions.

The institutional setting. – The term "institutional setting" is used here as a label for two different notions of institutions, namely "institutions-as-arenas" and "organizations-as-actors." The notion of *arena* seems to correspond to what Oran Young has called "the procedural component" of regimes, defined as "recognized practices for handling situations requiring social and collective choice" (Young, 1989, p. 18). Arenas regulate the access of actors to problems and the access of problems to decision games.

Moreover, they specify the official purpose as well as the rules, location, and timing of the game. Institutions-as-arenas can be described by answering the question: *Who* are to deal with *which* problem(s), *how, when,* and *where*?

Arenas differ in terms of, *inter alia,* rules of access, decision rules, and rules of procedure. For example, membership is in some cases restricted to countries that satisfy certain criteria (as is the case with, for example, the Antarctic Treaty System). Other organizations (for example the International Whaling Commission) are open to any state that cares to submit a formal application and pay its membership fee.[12] The rules of access to particular (executive) bodies will often be more restrictive than the criteria for membership of the organization as such. Consensus is the decision rule most frequently subscribed to in intergovernmental organizations (IGOs), but a number of organizations have some provisions for decision-making by voting (usually qualified majority for substantive decisions). The decision rule is clearly an important determinant of the capacity to aggregate diverging preferences; other things being equal, aggregation capacity reaches its maximum in strictly hierarchical strructures, and is at its minimum in systems requiring agreement (unanimity). Lastly, we know that procedural arrangements may differ in several respects, for example with regard to differentiation into subprocesses (committee work vs. plenary sessions), and the amount of discretion vested in committee or conference chairs in, *inter alia,* drafting proposals ("negotiating texts").

One important research question generated by these observations becomes: To what extent and how do different rules and arrangements affect the capabilities of institutions-as-arenas to fulfill certain critical functions in the decision-making process – including those of providing actors with incentives to adopt and pursue a "constructive" problem-solving approach, providing procedural opportunities for transcending initial constraints (for example by coupling or de-coupling issues), and enhancing the institutional capacity to integrate or aggregate actor preferences?

Providing incentives to adopt a constructive problem-solving approach is no trivial function. Inherent in the process of distributive bargaining are certain "perversities," providing "incentives to actors to behave in ways that have the effect of hindering mutually beneficial cooperation" (Keohane, 1988, p. 29). One well-known economist has taken the argument one step further by formulating what might be called "the iron law of bargaining," saying that inherent in the process of (distributive) bargaining is a severe risk of spoiling or blocking the integrative potential that it is ostensibly undertaken to tap (Johansen, 1979). One of these "perversities" is the temptation to hold back or distort relevant information. Another is the temptation to exploit the good faith of one's prospective partners (for example by "cheating"). A third is the development of "process-generated stakes," introducing a bias in favor of behavior that is believed to look good in the eyes of domestic clients and interested third parties, and increasing the risk that an actor may become trapped in his or her own commitments.

Such incentive distortions are hard to preclude or remove entirely, but procedural rules can make a significant difference. For one thing, institutionalization itself may help: incentives to deceive or exploit tend to be stronger in a one-time encounter than in a more permanent relationship providing multiple opportunities for retaliation (see for example Axelrod and Keohane, 1985, pp. 232f). Building institutional capacity (in the form of, for instance, joint or independent commissions of experts) for the production of reliable and consensual knowledge can dispel or weaken incentives to hold back or distort information, and reduce the fear of being misled by one's opponent. Among the organizational measures that can be taken to control process-generated stakes are provisions for confidential and exploratory talks (Druckman, 1973, p. 46), provisions for the active leadership or mediative services of "systemic actors" such as conference chairs, and steps to dismantle or bypass contested symbols. Moreover, splitting up negotiations into subprocesses or negotiating issues within the context of some established body imbued with a strong professional culture may offer some protection against "contamination" from particularly sensitive "external" issues. Organizational tools may be used for more offensive purposes as well. Thus, one of the basic propositions of (neo)functionalist theories of integration is that the structuring of the agenda can be used as an instrument for building up positive momentum (Haas, 1958; see also Walton and McKersie, 1965, p. 171; Rothstein, 1984, p. 323).

Second, the institutional setting should provide procedural opportunities for transcending initial constraints as well as physical and technical facilities for efficient work. The former requires first and foremost a flexible agenda (Walton and McKersie, 1965, pp. 151–2), permitting what Sebenius (1983) has referred to as the adding and subtraction of issues and parties. The quality of working conditions depends on a number of factors, ranging from the availability of suitable meeting and accommodation facilities via adequate technical support services to climatic "stress."

Lastly, the institutional setting should be designed with a view to providing capacity for integrating and aggregating actor interests and preferences. As the terms are being used here, "integrating" interests refers to the design of integrative solutions (i.e. solutions from which at least one actor gains and no partner loses). Here, the services of "systemic" actors or other entrepreneurs may be critical (see below). While the essence of integration is *combining* interests, aggregation is a matter of establishing priorities and cutting through bargaining deadlocks. Aggregation capacity is, then, determined essentially by the decision rule and the distribution of power.

Although all institutions can serve as arenas, only a subset can also qualify as significant actors in their own right. International organizations can be considered actors to the extent that they provide independent inputs into the problem-solving process or somehow amplify the output. To qualify as actor, an organization must have a certain minimum of internal coherence (unity), autonomy vis-à-vis other actors (notably member states), political resources, and external activity. International organizations, and even specific bodies within them, vary considerably in terms of scores on these dimensions. Thus, there is a substantial difference in actor capacity between the Commission of the European Communities and the secretariat of the International Whaling Commission. In general, the stronger the capacity of institutions such as conference presidents and organization secretariats to undertake independent initiatives or in some other way to "act" politically, the more institutional energy will presumably be available for pursuing "the common good."[13]

The distribution of power. – The more demanding the decision rule, the more critical becomes leadership of some kind. And, the less formal authority that is vested in the conference chair and the secretariat, the more important become informal sources of power.

Following Coleman (1973), two "faces" of power may be distinguished. One derives from control over events important to *oneself*, the other from control over events important to *others*. The former provides autonomy – the privilege of being able to pursue one's own interest without having to worry about what others might want to do. The latter provides an actor with the means to impose their will on others. The notion of "hegemony" combines the two (see, for example, Snidal, 1985). The "benevolent" hegemon is an actor sufficiently predominant to be able and willing to provide collective goods at their own expense, or – more generally – to establish and maintain unilateral solutions to collective problems. By contrast, the "coercive" hegemon rules by virtue of their control over events important to others, and they use this control to induce (submissive) cooperation. Either way, power can be a device to break aggregation deadlocks. We may therefore conclude that, other things being equal, the more "unipolar" the distribution of power in a system, the greater its capacity to aggregate diverging preferences,[14] and the more likely it is that *some* solution (unilateral or joint) will be developed and in fact also implemented.[15]

Skill and energy. – The third constitutive element in this conceptualization of problem-solving capacity – skill and energy – takes us beyond the study of "structural" characteristics and into the study of behavior. The kinds of skill and energy most relevant in this context are those that go into the "political engineering" of international cooperation; more specifically those that pertain to the design of substantive solutions, the design of institutional arrangements through which "good" solutions can be identified, adopted, and implemented, and the development of actor strategies that are effective in inducing the constructive cooperation of prospective partners. I have explored some aspects of the impact of institutional arrangements above; suffice it here to add some brief remarks about the "craft" of designing substantive solutions.

To qualify as *good*, a solution to a collective problem should meet several substantive criteria – notably effectiveness, efficiency, fairness, and feasibility. Again using the problem of environmental degradation as an illustration, a "good" solution should first of all induce behavior that is ecologically "sound." Second, a regime should induce resource allocations that are economically efficient. Not all ecologically sound regimes will do so. A "good" solution should also distribute costs and benefits in a way that is considered "fair," and there is *a priori* no reason to assume that an efficient solution will also be fair. Lastly, if a solution is not only to be invented but also to be established and implemented, it should be feasible – politically as well as technically. One important challenge for political science research is to formulate precisely the principles that we shall have to observe in identifying or designing politically feasible solutions.

I have wrestled with the latter question elsewhere (Underdal, 1992). Suffice it here to point out that what can be accomplished through collective decision-making processes may be seen as a function of three major determinants: the institutional setting, the configuration of actor preferences, and the distribution of power. In exploring the feasibility of a particular solution, we normally accept all these factors as exogenously determined, and ask three main questions: (1) What are the *minimal* requirements that a solution should have to meet in order to be adopted and implemented in these circumstances? (2) What is the *maximum* that we can hope to accomplish? And, (3) how would we design a solution if our only concern were to maximize its chances of being adopted and implemented?[16] Assuming that joint solutions will have to pass the most demanding of all decision rules (unanimity), how would we answer these three questions?

According to what might be called "standard textbook wisdom," the *critical minimum* may be defined as follows. To be "adoptable," a solution must be considered integrative. A strongly integrative solution can be defined as one preferred by all parties to the best available alternative that is unilaterally accessible (BATNA), while a weakly integrative option is one preferred to BATNA by at least one party and not considered inferior to any other accessible solution by any prospective partner. When three or more actors are involved, the answer becomes slightly more complex. To be established by consensus among a given set of actors $(N > 2)$, a solution must not only be integrative but also belong to the "core," i.e. not be inferior to any solution that can be established by some subgroup of actors (see, for example, Riker and Ordeshook, 1973, p. 134). To be successfully implemented as well, a solution must also be able to "survive" the encounter with the problem it has been designed to solve. A solution satisfying this requirement is said to be "stable." The stability of a cooperative arrangement depends in essence on the extent to which incentives to defect are absent or effectively curbed.

The *maximum* that one can hope to achieve through agreement is a Pareto-optimal solution. This frontier is reached whenever further improvement for one party can take place only at the expense of one or more of its prospective partners.

The general receipe for *maximizing political feasibility* is to design a solution so that marginal net gain is allocated wherever it contributes most to increasing the aggregate relative power of the set of actors supporting the option in question. In the special case where decisions are to be made through agreement among parties equal in power, political feasibility will be maximized when marginal cost is distributed in proportion to marginal gain (Olson, 1968, pp. 30–1).

Instead of asking what characterizes the set of solutions on which a given set of actors can agree, we might ask what characterizes the set of solutions that can *somehow* – i. e. by *any* set of actors – be established through voluntary cooperation (see Hovi, 1988). The answer to the latter question will, of course, differ from that given to the former only in cases where a particular solution can be established also by some subset of actors. Fortunately, such a possibility does sometimes exist, even for global environmental problems. In order to determine whether or not a particular solution can feasibly be established by a subset of actors we must be able to identify the set of *pivotal* actors and their preferences. Within this set of pivotal actors, the minimal requirements indicated above apply.

Now, these "standard textbook answers" all build on a simplistic conception of negotiation as a "politics-free" game whereby unitary rational actors make a collective choice from a given set of options. In trying to design politically feasible solutions, a political entrepreneur should therefore observe some important caveats.

First of all, equating the critical minimum that an actor will settle for with the best solution that is otherwise accessible (i.e. their BATNA) may lead us to *under*estimate the challenge we are facing. Governments typically enter international negotiations with some more or less clear idea of what will qualify as a "satisfactory" outcome. Such subjective aspirations seem to provide an important standard of evaluation, and it is not *a priori* obvious that an actor will be ready to accept a solution that offers a marginal improvement over BATNA if that solution fails to meet their "satisfaction standard."

Second, preferring one solution to their BATNA does not necessarily imply that the actor will also be ready to *accept* that solution, let alone propose it. For one thing, as Fred C. Iklé (1964) reminded us, an actor most of the time has a "three-fold choice": accept the terms presently available, reject the opponent's offer and withdraw, and continue the search for a better deal. Moreover, the acts of accepting or proposing may themselves have some stakes attached. If, for example, a particular deal fails to meet the government's aspirations or those of its domestic clients, the government may very well find that the act of explicitly accepting that particular solution entails political costs that outweigh the marginal improvement in substantive terms over BATNA. In such a situation it could be perfectly sensible *not* to settle for a solution that the actor would – had the solution been considered on its own merits only – prefer to their BATNA. One important implication of this proposition is that designing feasible solutions is only one component of the entrepreneurial challenge; the entrepreneur may also have to devise a path that can actually lead actors towards that solution. The latter task may certainly be as intricate as the former.

Finally, while the players portrayed in formal bargaining theory face a problem of making a joint *choice* of one particular solution from a predetermined set of options, actors in international negotiations typically enter with incomplete and imperfect information, and perhaps also with tentative and vague preferences. This implies that *discovering, inventing,* and *exploring* possible solutions may be important elements of the process, and – accordingly – also major challenges for the political entrepreneur.

The basic assumption underlying the argument in this section can now be summarized in a very simple proposition: Other things being equal, the more skill and energy that can be geared to such tasks of entrepreneurial leadership, the greater will be the problem-solving capacity of the system.

A brief note on "explanatory power"

I strongly suspect that the character of the problem would account for most of the variance in "success" that could in fact be observed in almost any survey of actual cases. Support for this hypothesis would not, however, necessarily imply that problem "benignity" is, in a basic sense, a more important determinant of regime effectiveness than "problem-solving capacity." Such a conclusion would be warranted only if both independent variables were measured by the same yardstick. This is a requirement that we cannot meet; obviously, we cannot claim that one unit of "benignity" *equals* one unit of "problem-solving capacity."[17] The amount of variation accounted for by a given independent variable is a function of its relative basic weight and its range of actual variation in a sample of observations. In the absence of a standardized unit of measurement, we have no firm basis for distinguishing the impact of the former from that of the latter.

Acknowledgements

Section 2 of this paper is reproduced, with minor changes, from my article "The Concept of Regime 'Effectiveness'," published in *Cooperation and Conflict*, vol. 27 (1992), no. 3, with permission of the editor and Sage Publications. I gratefully acknowledge useful comments on an earlier version from the editor of this volume. Moreover, I have benefited substantially from discussing some of the ideas outlined in this article with several other scholars, including Steinar Andresen, Robert O. Keohane, Edward L. Miles, Oran R. Young, and Jørgen Wettestad.

Notes

1 Aggarwal (1985, p. 20) defines regime "strength" according to "the stringency with which rules regulate the behavior of countries." Zacker (1987, p. 177) suggests that "the *strength* of a regime should be determined by the extent to which the package of injunctions constrains states' behavior."

2 Compare the definition adopted by Aggarwal with that proposed by Haggard and Simmons (1987, p. 496): "Strength is measured by the degree of compliance with regime injunctions." I can see no basis for assuming a straightforward positive link between "stringency" or "constraints" on the one hand and compliance on the other; in fact, one might suspect that – *ceteris paribus* – compliance would tend to be easier and therefore also higher the *less* stringent the rules and the *less* significant the constraints upon state behavior.

3 Sometimes, a distinction should also be made between the *outcome* of a regulation (i.e. its impact on the behavior of those to whom it applies) and the *impact* of those behavioral changes on the state of the environment.

4 "Effectiveness" measured in terms of impact thus implies a requirement of robustness or stability; a regime must, at the very least, be able to survive the encounter with the problem it has been designed to solve. More generally, a solution is normally considered "stable" to the extent that incentives to defect or cheat are absent or effectively curbed.

5 Note that our choice of evaluation standard may imply a choice of object as well. Thus, if we decide to evaluate regimes against some notion of political feasibility, output seems to be the appropriate object.

6 This formulation does not imply an assumption that a new regime will *necessarily* improve the present state of affairs. Presumably, improving collective outcomes will be the rationale behind the establishment or restructuring of a regime. There is no sound basis for assuming, however, that a new regime will in fact necessarily function as intended by its creators. As conceived of here, then, "relative improvement" – at least if measured in terms of *impact* – can be *negative* as well as *positive*.

7 This is an important proviso. If a group of actors succeed in accomplishing all that could be accomplished given the best knowledge available by the time, any distance remaining to the "objective" collective optimum would be a failure of *knowledge-making* rather than of *decision-making*. To a student of politics, the latter will be the more important concern.

8 We do realize that this formulation leads into intriguing conceptual problems if we accept the claim made by Puchala and Hopkins (1982, p. 247) that "a regime exists in every substantive issue-area in international relations where there is discernibly patterned behavior." The notion of a "no-regime" condition seems to require a stricter definition of "regime," notably one where the existence of *explicit* norms, rules, and procedures is considered a defining characteristic.

9 The choice between human welfare or ecological sustainability can be seen as a choice of evaluation *standard* as well, not merely as a choice of "metric." It goes without saying that there is a close link between evaluation standard and unit of measurement.

10 "Process effectiveness" is defined by Young as a matter of "the extent to which the provisions of an international regime are implemented in the domestic legal and political systems of the member states as well as the extent to which those subject to a regime's prescriptions comply with their requirements." A regime is effective in "constitutive" terms if "its formation gives rise to a social practice involving the expenditure of time, energy, and resources on the part of its members." The latter may seem a counter-intuitive notion of "effectiveness"; a somewhat unkind interpretation would be that the greater the social costs of operating a regime, the more "effective" it is.

11 A more elaborate analysis of problem "malignancy" can be found in Underdal (1987).

12 In fact, failure to pay membership fees seems *not* to imply automatic exclusion.

13 This is not to deny that conference chairs and secretariats may take advantage of their positions to pursue (also) their own private interests.

14 By implication, power is most useful the more "malign" the problem. Control over events important to others is a device for breaking the resistance of others, and autonomy is a necessary, but not sufficient, condition for opting for unilateral solutions.

15 Whether solutions established by unilateral action or imposed through coercive leadership will also be "optimal" or "fair" is a different question.

16 Note that these are *two* sets of requirements. Some of the techniques that can be used to facilitate agreement – e.g. despecification of commitments and issue linkage – tend to gloss over persistent disagreement that may become re-activated and strain the process of implementation. Moreover, in terms of domestic politics, the process is often a distinct "game," involving different actors with different perspectives on the issue.

17 We may add that this is not a shortcoming that we can hope to get around through further refinements of the conceptual framework; the problem seems in principle *unsolvable* – except in a purely statistical sense (by reconceptualizing explanatory power in terms of units of standard deviation).

References

Aggarwal, Vinod (1985) *Liberal Protectionism: The International Politics of Organized Textile Trade* (Berkeley: University of California Press).

Axelrod, Robert and Robert O. Keohane (1985) "Achieving Cooperation under Anarchy: Strategies and Institutions." *World Politics*, vol. 38, no. 1, pp. 226–54.

Coleman, James (1973) *The Mathematics of Collective Action* (London: Heineman).

Druckman, Daniel (1973) *Human Factors in International Negotiations: Social-Psychological Aspects of International Conflict* (Beverly Hills: Sage, Professional Paper in International Studies, 02-020).

Easton, David (1965) *A Systems Analysis of Political Life* (New York: John Wiley).

Haas, Ernst B. (1958) *The Uniting of Europe* (Stanford, Calif.: Stanford University Press).

Haggard, Stephan and Beth A. Simmons (1987) "Theories of International Regimes," *International Organization*, vol. 41, no. 3, pp. 491–517.

Hovi, Jon (1988) "Hvilke typer av prosjekter kan realiseres gjennom internasjonalt samarbeid?" *Internasjonal Politikk*, 1988/6, pp. 109–20.

Iklé, Fred C. (1964) *How Nations Negotiate* (New York: Harper & Row).

Jacobson, Harold K. and David A. Kay (1983) "Conclusions and Policy" in D. A. Kay and H. K. Jacobson, eds, *Environmental Protection: The International Dimension* (Totowa, NJ: Allanheld, Osmun), pp. 310–31.

Johansen, Leif (1979) "The Bargaining Society and the Inefficiency of Bargaining." *Kyklos*, vol. 32, pp. 497–522.

Kay, David A. and Harold K. Jacobson (1983) *Environmental Protection: The International Dimension* (Totowa, NJ: Allanheld, Osmun).

Keohane, Robert O. (1988) "Bargaining Perversities, Institutions and International Economic Relations," in Paolo Guerrieri and Pier Carlo Padoan, eds, *The Political Economy of International Co-operation* (London: Croom Helm), pp. 28–50.

Miles, Edward L. (1991) "Regime Effectiveness in Three Cases: Satellite Telecommunications, High Seas Salmon in the North Pacific, and Sea

Dumping of Low-Level Radioactive Waste," unpublished paper, prepared for the "Regime Summit", Dartmouth College, November.

Olson, Mancur (1968) *The Logic of Collective Action* (New York: Schocken Books; first published by Harvard University Press).

Puchala, Donald J., and Raymond F. Hopkins (1982) "International Regimes: Lessons from Inductive Analysis," *International Organization*, vol. 36, no. 2, pp. 245–75.

Riker, William H., and Peter C. Ordeshook (1973) *An Introduction to Positive Political Theory* (Englewood Cliffs, NJ: Prentice-Hall).

Rothstein, Robert L. (1984) "Regime-Creation by a Coalition of the Weak: Lessons from the NIEO and the Integrated Program for Commodities," *International Studies Quarterly*, vol. 28, no. 3, pp. 307–28.

Sebenius, James K. (1983) "Negotiation Arithmetic: Adding and Subtracting Issues and Parties," *International Organization*, vol. 37, no. 3, pp. 281–316.

Snidal, Duncan C. (1985). "The Limits of Hegemonic Stability Theory," *International Organization*, vol. 39, no. 4, pp. 579–614.

Underdal, Arild (1987) "International Cooperation: Transforming 'Needs' into 'Deeds'," *Journal of Peace Research*, vol. 27, no. 2, pp. 167–183.

Underdal, Arild (1992) "Designing Politically Feasible Solutions," i R. Malnes and A. Underdal, eds, *Rationality and Institutions* (Oslo: Scandinavian University Press).

Underdal, Arild (1994) "Progress in the Absence of Joint Solutions? Notes on the Dynamics of Regime Formation Processes," in Ted Hanisch, ed. *Climate Change and the Agenda for Research* (Boulder, Co: Westview).

Young, Oran R. (1989) *International Cooperation* (Ithaca, NY: Cornell University Press).

Young, Oran R. (1991) "On the Effectiveness of International Regimes: Defining Concepts and Identifying Variables," unpublished working paper prepared for use by the Dartmouth-based research team studying the effectiveness of international regimes.

Walton, Richard E., and Robert B. McKersie (1965) *A Behavioral Theory of Labor Negotiations* (New York: The Free Press).

Wettestad, Jørgen, and Steinar Andresen (1991) "The Effectiveness of International Resource Cooperation: Some Preliminary Findings," R:007-1991, the Fridtjof Nansen Institute, Lysaker.

Zacker, Mark W. (1987) "Trade Gaps, Analytical Gaps: Regime Analysis and International Commodity Trade Regulation," *International Organization*, vol. 41, no. 2, pp. 173–202.